BENEDICT ANDERSON was born in 1936 in Kunming, in the Yunnan province of China. He was educated at Cambridge University, where he studied Classics, and Cornell University, where he specialized in Indonesian studies. An Irish citizen, he is now Professor of Government and Asian Studies at Cornell University; and Associate Director of the Cornell Southeast Asia Program and Modern Indonesia Project. An editor of the journal *Indonesia*, he is the author of *Java in a Time of Revolution*, Ithaca 1972.

Imagined Communities

Reflections on the Origin and
Spread of Nationalism

◆

BENEDICT ANDERSON

VERSO

London · New York

First published 1983
Second impression 1985
Third impression 1986
Fourth impression 1987
Fifth impression 1989

Verso
UK: 6 Meard Street, London W1V 3HR
USA: 29 West 35th Street, New York, NY 10001-2291

Typeset in Garamond by Preface Ltd, Salisbury

Printed and bound in Great Britain by
Biddles Ltd, Guildford and King's Lynn

ISBN 0-86091-059-8
ISBN 0-86091-759-2 Pbk

Contents

Acknowledgments

As will be apparent to the reader, my thinking about nationalism has been deeply affected by the writings of Erich Auerbach, Walter Benjamin, and Victor Turner. In preparing the book itself, I have benefitted enormously from the criticism and advice of my brother Perry Anderson, Anthony Barnett, and Steve Heder. J. A. Ballard, Mohamed Chambas, Peter Katzenstein, the late Rex Mortimer, Francis Mulhern, Tom Nairn, Shiraishi Takashi, Jim Siegel, Laura Summers, and Esta Ungar also gave me invaluable help in different ways. Naturally, none of these friendly critics should be held in any way accountable for the text's deficiencies, which are wholly my responsibility. I should perhaps add that I am by training and profession a specialist on Southeast Asia. This admission may help to explain some of the book's biases and choices of examples, as well as to deflate its would-be-global pretensions.

ACKNOWLEDGEMENTS

For Mamma and Tantiette
in love and gratitude

He regards it as his task to brush history against the grain.

Walter Benjamin, *Illuminations*.

Thus from a Mixture of all kinds began,
That Het'rogeneous Thing, *An Englishman*:
In eager Rapes, and furious Lust begot,
Betwixt a Painted *Britton* and a *Scot*:
Whose gend'ring Offspring quickly learnt to bow,
And yoke their Heifers to the *Roman* Plough:
From whence a Mongrel half-bred Race there came,
With neither Name nor Nation, Speech or Fame.
In whose hot Veins new Mixtures quickly ran,
Infus'd betwixt a *Saxon* and a *Dane*.
While their Rank Daughters, to their Parents just,
Receiv'd all Nations with Promiscuous Lust.
This Nauseous Brood directly did contain
The well-extracted Blood of *Englishmen* . . . . .

From Daniel Defoe, *The True-Born Englishman*.

1
Introduction

Perhaps without being much noticed yet, a fundamental transformation in the history of Marxism and Marxist movements is upon us. Its most visible signs are the recent wars between Vietnam, Cambodia and China. These wars are of world-historical importance because they are the first to occur between regimes whose independence and revolutionary credentials are undeniable, and because none of the belligerents has made more than the most perfunctory attempts to justify the bloodshed in terms of a recogniz-able *Marxist* theoretical perspective. While it was still just possible to interpret the Sino-Soviet border clashes of 1969, and the Soviet military interventions in Germany (1953), Hungary (1956), Czechoslovakia (1968), and Afghanistan (1980) in terms of — according to taste — 'social imperial-ism,' 'defending socialism,' etc., no one, I imagine, seriously believes that such vocabularies have much bearing on what has occurred in Indochina.

If the Vietnamese invasion and occupation of Cambodia in December 1978 and January 1979 represented the first *large-scale conventional war* waged by one revolutionary Marxist regime against another,[1] China's

---

1. This formulation is chosen simply to emphasize the scale and the style of the fighting, not to assign blame. To avoid possible misunderstanding, it should be said that the December 1978 invasion grew out of armed clashes between partisans of the two revolutionary move-ments going back possibly as far as 1971. After April 1977, border raids, initiated by the Cambodians, but quickly followed by the Vietnamese, grew in size and scope, culminating in the major Vietnamese incursion of December 1977. None of these raids, however, aimed at overthrowing enemy regimes or occupying large territories, nor were the numbers of troops involved comparable to those deployed in December 1978. The controversy over the causes of the war is most thoughtfully pursued in: Stephen P. Heder, 'The Kampuchean-Vietnamese Conflict,' in David W. P. Elliott, ed., *The Third Indochina Conflict*, pp. 21–67; Anthony Barnett, 'Inter-Communist Conflicts and Vietnam,' *Bulletin of Concerned Asian Scholars*, 11: 4 (October–December 1979), pp. 2–9; and Laura Summers, 'In Matters of War and Socialism Anthony Barnett would Shame and Honour Kampuchea Too Much,' ibid., pp. 10–18.

assault on Vietnam in February rapidly confirmed the precedent. Only the most trusting would dare wager that in the declining years of this century any significant outbreak of inter-state hostilities will necessarily find the USSR and the PRC – let alone the smaller socialist states – supporting, or fighting on, the same side. Who can be confident that Yugoslavia and Albania will not one day come to blows? Those variegated groups who seek a withdrawal of the Red Army from its encampments in Eastern Europe should remind themselves of the degree to which its overwhelming presence has, since 1945, ruled out armed conflict between the region's Marxist regimes.

Such considerations serve to underline the fact that since World War II every successful revolution has defined itself in *national* terms – the People's Republic of China, the Socialist Republic of Vietnam, and so forth – and, in so doing, has grounded itself firmly in a territorial and social space inherited from the prerevolutionary past. Conversely, the fact that the Soviet Union shares with the United Kingdom of Great Britain and Northern Ireland the rare distinction of refusing nationality in its naming suggests that it is as much the legatee of the prenational dynastic states of the nineteenth century as the precursor of a twenty-first century internationalist order.[2]

Eric Hobsbawm is perfectly correct in stating that 'Marxist movements and states have tended to become national not only in form but in substance, i.e., nationalist. There is nothing to suggest that this trend will not continue.'[3] Nor is the tendency confined to the socialist world. Almost every year the United Nations admits new members. And many 'old nations,' once thought fully consolidated, find themselves challenged by 'sub'-nationalisms within their borders – nationalisms which, naturally, dream of shedding this sub-ness one happy day. The reality is quite plain: the 'end of the era of nationalism,' so long prophesied, is not remotely in sight. Indeed, nation-ness is the most universally legitimate value in the political life of our time.

But if the facts are clear, their explanation remains a matter of long-standing dispute. Nation, nationality, nationalism – all have proved notoriously difficult to define, let alone to analyse. In contrast to the

2. Anyone who has doubts about the UK's claims to such parity with the USSR should ask himself what nationality its name denotes: Great Brito-Irish?

3. Eric Hobsbawm, 'Some Reflections on "The Break-up of Britain"', *New Left Review*, 105 (September–October 1977), p. 13.

immense influence that nationalism has exerted on the modern world, plausible theory about it is conspicuously meagre. Hugh Seton-Watson, author of far the best and most comprehensive English-language text on nationalism, and heir to a vast tradition of liberal historiography and social science, sadly observes: 'Thus I am *driven* to the conclusion that no "scientific definition" of the nation can be devised; yet the phenomenon has existed and exists.'[4] Tom Nairn, author of the path-breaking *The Break-up of Britain*, and heir to the scarcely less vast tradition of Marxist historiography and social science, candidly remarks: 'The theory of nationalism represents Marxism's great historical failure.'[5] But even this confession is somewhat misleading, insofar as it can be taken to imply the regrettable outcome of a long, self-conscious search for theoretical clarity. It would be more exact to say that nationalism has proved an uncomfortable *anomaly* for Marxist theory and, precisely for that reason, has been largely elided, rather than confronted. How else to explain Marx's own failure to explicate the crucial pronoun in his memorable formulation of 1848: 'The proletariat of each country must, of course, first of all settle matters with *its own* bourgeoisie'?[6] How else to account for the use, for over a century, of the concept 'national bourgeoisie' without any serious attempt to justify theoretically the relevance of the adjective? Why is *this* segmentation of the bourgeoisie – a world-class insofar as it is defined in terms of the relations of production – theoretically significant?

The aim of this book is to offer some tentative suggestions for a more satisfactory interpretation of the 'anomaly' of nationalism. My sense is that on this topic both Marxist and liberal theory have become etiolated in a late Ptolemaic effort to 'save the phenomena'; and that a reorientation of perspective in, as it were, a Copernican spirit, is urgently required. My point of departure is that nationality, or, as one might prefer to put it in view of that word's multiple significations, nation-ness, as well as nationalism, are cultural artefacts of a particular kind. To understand them properly we need to consider carefully how they have come into historical being, in what ways their meanings have changed over time, and why, today, they

---

4. See his *Nations and States*, p. 5. Emphasis added.

5. See his 'The Modern Janus,' *New Left Review*, 94 (November–December 1975), p. 3. This essay is included unchanged in *The Break-up of Britain* as chapter 9 (pp. 329–63).

6. Karl Marx and Friedrich Engels, *The Communist Manifesto*, in the *Selected Works*, I, p. 45. Emphasis added. In any theoretical exegesis, the words 'of course' should flash red lights before the transported reader.

command such profound emotional legitimacy. I will be trying to argue that the creation of these artefacts towards the end of the eighteenth century[7] was the spontaneous distillation of a complex 'crossing' of discrete historical forces; but that, once created, they became 'modular,' capable of being transplanted, with varying degrees of self-consciousness, to a great variety of social terrains, to merge and be merged with a correspondingly wide variety of political and ideological constellations. I will also attempt to show why these particular cultural artefacts have aroused such deep attachments.

Concepts and Definitions

Before addressing the questions raised above, it seems advisable to consider briefly the concept of 'nation' and offer a workable definition. Theorists of nationalism have often been perplexed, not to say irritated, by these three paradoxes: 1. The objective modernity of nations to the historian's eye vs. their subjective antiquity in the eyes of nationalists. 2. The formal universality of nationality as a socio-cultural concept — in the modern world everyone can, should, will 'have' a nationality, as he or she 'has' a gender — vs. the irremediable particularity of its concrete manifestations, such that, by definition, 'Greek' nationality is sui generis. 3. The 'political' power of nationalisms vs. their philosophical poverty and even incoherence. In other words, unlike most other isms, nationalism has never produced its own grand thinkers: no Hobbeses, Tocquevilles, Marxes, or Webers. This 'emptiness' easily gives rise, among cosmopolitan and polylingual intellectuals, to a certain condescension. Like Gertrude Stein in the face of Oakland, one can rather quickly conclude that there is 'no there there'. It is characteristic that even so sympathetic a student of nationalism as Tom Nairn can nonetheless write that: '"Nationalism" is the pathology of modern developmental history, as inescapable as "neurosis" in the individual, with much the same essential ambiguity attaching to it, a similar built-in

---

7. As Aira Kemiläinen notes, the twin 'founding fathers' of academic scholarship on nationalism, Hans Kohn and Carleton Hayes, argued persuasively for this dating. Their conclusions have, I think, not been seriously disputed except by nationalist ideologues in particular countries. Kemiläinen also observes that the word 'nationalism' did not come into wide general use until the end of the nineteenth century. It did not occur, for example, in many standard nineteenth century lexicons. If Adam Smith conjured with the wealth of 'nations,' he meant by the term no more than 'societies' or 'states.' Aira Kemiläinen, *Nationalism*, pp. 10, 33, and 48–49.

capacity for descent into dementia, rooted in the dilemmas of helplessness thrust upon most of the world (the equivalent of infantilism for societies) and largely incurable.'[8]

Part of the difficulty is that one tends unconsciously to hypostasize the existence of Nationalism-with-a-big-N — rather as one might Age-with-a-capital-A — and then to classify 'it' as *an* ideology. (Note that if everyone has an age, Age is merely an analytical expression.) It would, I think, make things easier if one treated it as if it belonged with 'kinship' and 'religion,' rather than with 'liberalism' or 'fascism'.

In an anthropological spirit, then, I propose the following definition of the nation: it is an imagined political community — and imagined as both inherently limited and sovereign.

It is *imagined* because the members of even the smallest nation will never know most of their fellow-members, meet them, or even hear of them, yet in the minds of each lives the image of their communion.[9] Renan referred to this imagining in his suavely back-handed way when he wrote that 'Or l'essence d'une nation est que tous les individus aient beaucoup de choses en commun, et aussi que tous aient oublié bien des choses.'[10] With a certain ferocity Gellner makes a comparable point when he rules that 'Nationalism is not the awakening of nations to self-consciousness: it *invents* nations where they do not exist.'[11] The drawback to this formulation, however, is that Gellner is so anxious to show that nationalism masquerades under false pretences that he assimilates 'invention' to 'fabrication' and 'falsity,' rather than to 'imagining' and 'creation'. In this way he implies that 'true' communities exist which can be advantageously juxtaposed to nations. In fact, all communities larger than primordial villages of face-to-face contact (and perhaps even these) are imagined. Communities are to be distinguished, not by their falsity/ genuineness, but by the style in which they are imagined. Javanese villagers have always known that they are connected to people they have

8. *The Break-up of Britain*, p. 359.

9. Cf. Seton-Watson, *Nations and States*, p. 5: 'All that I can find to say is that a nation exists when a significant number of people in a community consider themselves to form a nation, or behave as if they formed one.' We may translate 'consider themselves' as 'imagine themselves.'

10. Ernest Renan, 'Qu'est-ce qu'une nation?' in *Œuvres Complètes*, 1, p. 892. He adds: 'tout citoyen français doit avoir oublié la Saint-Barthélemy, les massacres du Midi au XIIIe siècle. Il n'y a pas en France dix familles qui puissent fournir la preuve d'une origine franque . . .'

11. Ernest Gellner, *Thought and Change*, p. 169. Emphasis added.

never seen, but these ties were once imagined particularistically – as indefinitely stretchable nets of kinship and clientship. Until quite recently, the Javanese language had no word meaning the abstraction 'society'. We may today think of the French aristocracy of the *ancien régime* as a class; but surely it was imagined this way only very late. [12] To the question 'Who is the Comte de X?' the normal answer would have been, not 'a member of the aristocracy,' but 'the lord of X,' 'the uncle of the Baronne de Y,' or 'a client of the Duc de Z'.

The nation is imagined as *limited* because even the largest of them, encompassing perhaps a billion living human beings, has finite, if elastic, boundaries, beyond which lie other nations. No nation imagines itself coterminous with mankind. The most messianic nationalists do not dream of a day when all the members of the human race will join their nation in the way that it was possible, in certain epochs, for, say, Christians to dream of a wholly Christian planet.

It is imagined as *sovereign* because the concept was born in an age in which Enlightenment and Revolution were destroying the legitimacy of the divinely-ordained, hierarchical dynastic realm. Coming to maturity at a stage of human history when even the most devout adherents of any universal religion were inescapably confronted with the living *pluralism* of such religions, and the allomorphism between each faith's ontological claims and territorial stretch, nations dream of being free, and, if under God, directly so. The gage and emblem of this freedom is the sovereign state.

Finally, it is imagined as a *community*, because, regardless of the actual inequality and exploitation that may prevail in each, the nation is always conceived as a deep, horizontal comradeship. Ultimately it is this fraternity that makes it possible, over the past two centuries, for so many millions of people, not so much to kill, as willingly to die for such limited imaginings.

These deaths bring us abruptly face to face with the central problem posed by nationalism: what makes the shrunken imaginings of recent history (scarcely more than two centuries) generate such colossal sacrifices? I believe that the beginnings of an answer lie in the cultural roots of nationalism.

12. Hobsbawm, for example, 'fixes' it by saying that in 1789 it numbered about 400,000 in a population of 23,000,000. (See his *The Age of Revolution*, p. 78). But would this statistical picture of the noblesse have been imaginable under the *ancien régime*?

2
Cultural Roots

No more arresting emblems of the modern culture of nationalism exist than cenotaphs and tombs of Unknown Soldiers. The public ceremonial reverence accorded these monuments precisely *because* they are either deliberately empty or no one knows who lies inside them, has no true precedents in earlier times.[1] To feel the force of this modernity one has only to imagine the general reaction to the busy-body who 'discovered' the Unknown Soldier's name or insisted on filling the cenotaph with some real bones. Sacrilege of a strange, contemporary kind! Yet void as these tombs are of identifiable mortal remains or immortal souls, they are nonetheless saturated with ghostly *national* imaginings.[2] (This is why so many different nations have such tombs without feeling any need to specify the nationality of their absent occupants. What else could they be *but* Germans, Americans, Argentinians . . .?)

The cultural significance of such monuments becomes even clearer if one tries to imagine, say, a Tomb of the Unknown Marxist or a cenotaph for

1. The ancient Greeks had cenotaphs, but for specific, known individuals whose bodies, for one reason or another, could not be retrieved for regular burial. I owe this information to my Byzantinist colleague Judith Herrin.
2. Consider, for example, these remarkable tropes: 1. 'The long grey line has never failed us. Were you to do so, a million ghosts in olive drab, in brown khaki, in blue and grey, would rise from their white crosses, thundering those magic words: Duty, honour, country.' 2. 'My estimate of [the American man-at-arms] was formed on the battlefield many, many years ago, and has never changed. I regarded him then, as I regard him now, as one of the world's noblest figures; not only as one of the finest military characters, but also as one of the most stainless [sic] . . . . He belongs to history as furnishing one of the greatest examples of successful patriotism [sic]. He belongs to posterity as the instructor of future generations in the principles of liberty and freedom. He belongs to the present, to us, by his virtues and his achievements.' Douglas MacArthur, 'Duty, Honour, Country,' Address to the U.S. Military Academy, West Point, May 12, 1962, in his *A Soldier Speaks*, pp. 354 and 357.

fallen Liberals. Is a sense of absurdity avoidable? The reason is that neither Marxism nor Liberalism are much concerned with death and immortality. If the nationalist imagining is so concerned, this suggests a strong affinity with religious imaginings. As this affinity is by no means fortuitous, it may be useful to begin a consideration of the cultural roots of nationalism with death, as the last of a whole gamut of fatalities.

If the manner of a man's dying usually seems arbitrary, his mortality is inescapable. Human lives are full of such combinations of necessity and chance. We are all aware of the contingency and ineluctability of our particular genetic heritage, our gender, our life-era, our physical capabilities, our mother-tongue, and so forth. The great merit of traditional religious world-views (which naturally must be distinguished from their role in the legitimation of specific systems of domination and exploitation) has been their concern with man-in-the-cosmos, man as species being, and the contingency of life. The extraordinary survival over thousands of years of Buddhism, Christianity or Islam in dozens of different social formations attests to their imaginative response to the overwhelming burden of human suffering — disease, mutilation, grief, age, and death. Why was I born blind? Why is my best friend paralysed? Why is my daughter retarded? The religions attempt to explain. The great weakness of all evolutionary/progressive styles of thought, not excluding Marxism, is that such questions are answered with impatient silence.[3] At the same time, in different ways, religious thought also responds to obscure intimations of immortality, generally by transforming fatality into continuity (karma, original sin, etc.) In this way, it concerns itself with the links between the dead and the yet unborn, the mystery of re-generation. Who experiences *their* child's conception and birth without dimly apprehending a combined connectedness, fortuity, and fatality in a language of 'con-

3. Cf. Régis Debray. 'Marxism and the National Question,' *New Left Review*, 105 (September–October 1977), p. 29. In the course of doing fieldwork in Indonesia in the 1960s I was struck by the calm refusal of many Muslims to accept the ideas of Darwin. At first I interpreted this refusal as obscurantism. Subsequently I came to see it as an honourable attempt to be consistent: the doctrine of evolution was simply not compatible with the teachings of Islam. What are we to make of a scientific materialism which formally accepts the findings of physics about matter, yet makes so little effort to link these findings with the class struggle, revolution, or whatever. Does not the abyss between protons and the proletariat conceal an unacknowledged metaphysical conception of man? But see the refreshing texts of Sebastiano Timpanaro, *On Materialism* and *The Freudian Slip*; and Raymond Williams' thoughtful response to them in 'Timpanaro's Materialist Challenge,' *New Left Review*, 109 (May–June 1978), pp. 3–17.

tinuity'? (Again, the disadvantage of evolutionary/progressive thought is an almost Heraclitean hostility to any idea of continuity.)

I bring up these perhaps simpleminded observations primarily because in Western Europe the eighteenth century marks not only the dawn of the age of nationalism but the dusk of religious modes of thought. The century of the Enlightenment, of rationalist secularism, brought with it its own modern darkness. With the ebbing of religious belief, the suffering which belief in part composed did not disappear. Disintegration of paradise: nothing makes fatality more arbitrary. Absurdity of salvation: nothing makes another style of continuity more necessary. What then was required was a secular transformation of fatality into continuity, contingency into meaning. As we shall see, few things were (are) better suited to this end than an idea of nation. If nation-states are widely conceded to be 'new' and 'historical,' the nations to which they give political expression always loom out of an immemorial past,[4] and, still more important, glide into a limitless future. It is the magic of nationalism to turn chance into destiny. With Debray we might say, 'Yes, it is quite accidental that I am born French; but after all, France is eternal.'

Needless to say, I am not claiming that the appearance of nationalism towards the end of the eighteenth century was 'produced' by the erosion of religious certainties, or that this erosion does not itself require a complex explanation. Nor am I suggesting that somehow nationalism historically 'supersedes' religion. What I am proposing is that nationalism has to be understood by aligning it, not with self-consciously held political ideologies, but with the large cultural systems that preceded it, out of which – as well as against which – it came into being.

4. The late President Sukarno always spoke with complete sincerity of the 350 years of colonialism that his 'Indonesia' had endured, although the very concept 'Indonesia' is a twentieth-century invention, and most of today's Indonesia was only conquered by the Dutch between 1850 and 1910. Preeminent among contemporary Indonesia's national heroes is the early nineteenth-century Javanese Prince Diponegoro, although the Prince's own memoirs show that he intended to 'conquer ⌊not liberate!⌋ *Java*,' rather than expel 'the Dutch.' Indeed, he clearly had no concept of 'the Dutch' as a collectivity. See Harry J. Benda and John A. Larkin, eds., *The World of Southeast Asia*, p. 158; and Ann Kumar, 'Diponegoro (1778?–1855),' *Indonesia*, 13 (April 1972), p. 103. Emphasis added. Similarly, Kemal Atatürk named one of his state banks the Eti Banka (Hittite Bank) and another the Sumerian Bank. (Seton-Watson, *Nations and States*, p. 259). These banks flourish today, and there is no reason to doubt that many Turks, possibly not excluding Kemal himself, seriously saw, and see, in the Hittites and Sumerians their Turkish forebears. Before laughing too hard, we should remind ourselves of Arthur and Boadicea, and ponder the commercial success of Tolkien's mythographies

For present purposes, the two relevant cultural systems are the *religious community* and the *dynastic realm*. For both of these, in their heydays, were taken-for-granted frames of reference, very much as nationality is today. It is therefore essential to consider what gave these cultural systems their self-evident plausibility, and at the same time to underline certain key elements in their decomposition.

The Religious Community

Few things are more impressive than the vast territorial stretch of the Ummah Islam from Morocco to the Sulu Archipelago, of Christendom from Paraguay to Japan, and of the Buddhist world from Sri Lanka to the Korean peninsula. The great sacral cultures (and for our purposes here it may be permissible to include 'Confucianism') incorporated conceptions of immense communities. But Christendom, the Ummah Islam, and even the Middle Kingdom — which, though we think of it today as Chinese, imagined itself not as Chinese, but as central — were imaginable largely through the medium of a sacred language and written script. Take only the example of Islam: if Maguindanao met Berbers in Mecca, knowing nothing of each other's languages, incapable of communicating orally, they nonetheless understood each other's ideographs, *because* the sacred texts they shared existed only in classical Arabic. In this sense, written Arabic functioned like Chinese characters to create a community out of signs, not sounds. (So today mathematical language continues an old tradition. Of what the Thai call + Rumanians have no idea, and vice versa, but both comprehend the symbol.) All the great classical communities conceived of themselves as cosmically central, through the medium of a sacred language linked to a superterrestrial order of power. Accordingly, the stretch of written Latin, Pali, Arabic, or Chinese was, in theory, unlimited. (In fact, the deader the written language — the farther it was from speech — the better: in principle everyone has access to a pure world of signs.)

Yet such classical communities linked by sacred languages had a character distinct from the imagined communities of modern nations. One crucial difference was the older communities' confidence in the unique sacredness of their languages, and thus their ideas about admission to membership. Chinese mandarins looked with approval on barbarians who painfully learned to paint Middle Kingdom ideograms. These barbarians were already halfway to full absorption.[5] Half-civilized was vastly better than barbarian. Such an attitude was certainly not peculiar to the Chinese, nor confined to antiquity. Consider, for example, the following 'policy on barbarians' formulated by the early-nineteenth-century Colombian liberal Pedro Fermín de Vargas:

> To expand our agriculture it would be necessary to hispanicize our Indians. Their idleness, stupidity, and indifference towards normal human endeavours causes one to think that they come from a degenerate race which deteriorates in proportion to the distance from its origin . . . *it would be very desirable that the Indians be extinguished, by miscegenation with the whites, declaring them free of tribute and other charges, and giving them private property in land.*[6]

How striking it is that this liberal still proposes to 'extinguish' his Indians in part by 'declaring them free of tribute' and 'giving them private property in land', rather than extermining them by gun and microbe as his heirs in Brazil, Argentina, and the United States began to do soon afterwards. Note also, alongside the condescending cruelty, a cosmic optimism: the Indian is ultimately redeemable — by impregnation with white, 'civilized' semen, and the acquisition of private property, *like everyone else.* (How different Fermín's attitude is from the later European imperialist's preference for 'genuine' Malays, Gurkhas, and Hausas over 'half-breeds', 'semi-educated natives', 'wogs,' and the like.)

Yet if the sacred silent languages were the media through which the great global communities of the past were imagined, the reality of such apparitions depended on an idea largely foreign to the contemporary Western mind: the non-arbitrariness of the sign. The ideograms of Chinese, Latin, or Arabic were emanations of reality, not randomly fabricated representations of it. We are familiar with the long dispute over the appropriate language (Latin or vernacular) for the mass. In the Islamic tradition, until quite recently, the Qur'an was literally untranslatable (and therefore untranslated), because Allah's truth was accessible only through the unsubstitutable true signs of written Arabic. There is no idea here of a world so separated from language that all languages are equidistant (and thus interchangeable) signs for it. In effect, ontological reality is apprehensible only

5. Hence the equanimity with which Sinicized Mongols and Manchus were accepted as Sons of Heaven.
6. John Lynch, *The Spanish-American Revolutions, 1808–1826*, p. 260. Emphasis added.

through a single, privileged system of re-presentation: the truth-language of Church Latin, Qur'anic Arabic, or Examination Chinese.[7] And, as truth-languages, imbued with an impulse largely foreign to nationalism, the impulse towards conversion. By conversion, I mean not so much the acceptance of particular religious tenets, but alchemic absorption. The barbarian becomes 'Middle Kingdom', the Rif Muslim, the Ilongo Christian. The whole nature of man's being is sacrally malleable. (Contrast thus the prestige of these old world-languages, towering high over all vernaculars, with Esperanto or Volapük, which lie ignored between them.) It was, after all, this possibility of conversion through the sacred language that made it possible for an 'Englishman' to become Pope[8] and a 'Manchu' Son of Heaven.

But even though the sacred languages made such communities as Christendom imaginable, the actual scope and plausibility of these communities can not be explained by sacred script alone: their readers were, after all, tiny literate reefs on top of vast illiterate oceans.[9] A fuller explanation requires a glance at the relationship between the literati and their societies. It would be a mistake to view the former as a kind of theological technocracy. The languages they sustained, if abstruse, had none of the self-arranged abstruseness of lawyers' or economists' jargons, on the margin of society's idea of reality. Rather, the literati were adepts, strategic strata in a cosmological hierarchy of which the apex was divine.[10] The fundamental conceptions about 'social groups' were centripetal and hierarchical, rather than boundary-oriented and horizontal. The astonishing power of the papacy in its noonday is only comprehensible in terms of a trans-European Latin-writing clerisy, *and* a conception of the world, shared by virtually

7. Church Greek seems not to have achieved the status of a truth-language. The reasons for this 'failure' are various, but one key factor was certainly the fact that Greek remained a *living* demotic speech (unlike Latin) in much of the Eastern Empire. This insight I owe to Judith Herrin.

8. Nicholas Brakespear held the office of pontiff between 1154 and 1159 under the name Adrian IV.

9. Marc Bloch reminds us that 'the majority of lords and many great barons [in mediaeval times] were administrators incapable of studying personally a report or an account.' *Feudal Society*, I, p. 81.

10. This is not to say that the illiterate did not read. What they read, however, was not words but the visible world. 'In the eyes of all who were capable of reflection the material world was scarcely more than a sort of mask, behind which took place all the really important things; it seemed to them also a language, intended to express by signs a more profound reality.' Bloch, p. 83.

everyone, that the bilingual intelligentsia, by mediating between vernacular and Latin, mediated between earth and heaven. (The awesomeness of excommunication reflects this cosmology.)

Yet for all the grandeur and power of the great religiously-imagined communities, their *unselfconscious coherence* waned steadily after the late Middle Ages. Among the reasons for this decline, I wish here to emphasize only the two which are directly related to these communities' unique sacredness.

First was the effect of the explorations of the non-European world, which mainly, but by no means exclusively, in Europe 'abruptly widened the cultural and geographic horizon and hence also men's conception of possible forms of human life.'[11] The process is already apparent in the greatest of all European travel-books. Consider the following awed description of Kublai Khan by the good Venetian Christian Marco Polo at the end of the thirteenth century:[12]

> The grand khan, having obtained this signal victory, returned with great pomp and triumph to the capital city of Kanbalu. This took place in the month of November, and he continued to reside there during the months of February and March, in which latter was *our* festival of Easter. Being aware that this was one of *our* principal solemnities, he commanded all the Christians to attend him, and to bring with them *their* Book, which contains the four Gospels of the Evangelists. After causing it to be repeatedly perfumed with incense, in a ceremonious manner, he devoutly kissed it, and directed that the same should be done by all his nobles who were present. This was his usual practice upon each of the principal Christian festivals, such as Easter and Christmas; and he observed the same at the festivals of the Saracens, Jews, and idolaters. Upon being asked his motive for this conduct, he said: 'There are four great Prophets who are reverenced and worshipped by the different classes of mankind. The Christians regard Jesus Christ as their divinity; the Saracens, Mahomet; the Jews, Moses; and the idolaters, Sogomombar-kan, the most eminent among their idols. I do honour and show respect to all the four, and invoke to my aid *whichever amongst them is in truth supreme in heaven.*' But from the manner in which his majesty acted towards them, it is evident that he regarded the faith of the Christians as the truest and the best . . . .

What is so remarkable about this passage is not so much the great Mongol dynast's calm religious relativism (it is still a *religious* relativism),

11. Erich Auerbach, *Mimesis*, p. 282.

12. Marco Polo, *The Travels of Marco Polo*, pp. 158–59. Emphases added. Notice that, though kissed, the Evangel is not read.

as Marco Polo's attitude and language. It never occurs to him, even though he is writing for fellow-European Christians, to term Kublai a hypocrite or an idolater. (No doubt in part because 'in respect to number of subjects, extent of territory, and amount of revenue, he surpasses every sovereign that has heretofore been or that now is in the world.')[13] And in the unselfconscious use of 'our' (which becomes 'their'), and the description of the faith of the Christians as 'truest', rather than 'true,' we can detect the seeds of a territorialization of faiths which foreshadows the language of many nationalists ('our' nation is 'the best' – in a competitive, *comparative field*).

What a revealing contrast is provided by the opening of the letter written by the Persian traveller 'Rica' to his friend 'Ibben' from Paris in '1712':[14]

> The Pope is the chief of the Christians; he is an ancient idol, worshipped now from habit. Once he was formidable even to princes, for he would depose them as easily as our magnificent sultans depose the kings of Iremetia or Georgia. But nobody fears him any longer. He claims to be the successor of one of the earliest Christians, called Saint Peter, and it is certainly a rich succession, for his treasure is immense and he has a great country under his control.

The deliberate, sophisticated fabrications of the eighteenth century Catholic mirror the naive realism of his thirteenth-century predecessor, but by now the 'relativization' and 'territorialization' are utterly selfconscious, and political in intent. Is it unreasonable to see a paradoxical elaboration of this evolving tradition in the Ayatollah Ruhollah Khomeini's identification of The Great Satan, not as a heresy, nor even as a demonic personage (dim little Carter scarcely fitted the bill), but as a *nation*?

Second was a gradual demotion of the sacred language itself. Writing of mediaeval Western Europe, Bloch noted that 'Latin was not only the language in which teaching was done, it was the *only language taught*.'[15] (This second 'only' shows quite clearly the sacredness of Latin – no other language was thought worth the teaching.) But by the sixteenth century all this was changing fast. The reasons for the change need not detain us here: the central importance of print-capitalism will be discussed below. It is suffi-

---

13. *The Travels of Marco Polo*, p. 152.

14. Henri de Montesquieu, *Persian Letters*, p. 81. The *Lettres Persanes* first appeared in 1721.

15. Bloch, *Feudal Society*, I, p. 77. Emphasis added.

cient to remind ourselves of its scale and pace. Febvre and Martin estimate that 77% of the books printed before 1500 were still in Latin (meaning nonetheless that 23% were already in vernaculars).[16] If of the 88 editions printed in Paris in 1501 all but 8 were in Latin, after 1575 a majority were always in French.[17] Despite a temporary come-back during the Counter-Reformation, Latin's hegemony was doomed. Nor are we speaking simply of a general popularity. Somewhat later, but at no less dizzying speed, Latin ceased to be the language of a pan-European high intelligentsia. In the seventeenth century Hobbes (1588–1678) was a figure of continental renown because he wrote in the truth-language. Shakespeare (1564–1616), on the other hand, composing in the vernacular, was virtually unknown across the Channel.[18] And had English not become, two hundred years later, the pre-eminent world-imperial language, might he not largely have retained his original insular obscurity? Meanwhile, these men's cross-Channel near-contemporaries, Descartes (1596–1650) and Pascal (1623–1662) conducted most of their correspondence in Latin; but virtually all of Voltaire's (1694–1778) was in the vernacular.[19] 'After 1640, with fewer and fewer books coming out in Latin, and more and more in the vernacular languages, publishing was ceasing to be an international [sic] enterprise.'[20] In a word, the fall of Latin exemplified a larger process in which the sacred communities integrated by old sacred languages were gradually fragmented, pluralized, and territorialized.

The Dynastic Realm

These days it is perhaps difficult to put oneself empathetically into a world in which the dynastic realm appeared for most men as the only imaginable 'political' system. For in fundamental ways 'serious' monarchy lies transverse to all modern conceptions of political life. Kingship organizes everything around a high centre. Its legitimacy derives from divinity, not from

16. Lucien Febvre and Henri-Jean Martin, *The Coming of the Book*, pp. 248–49.
17. Ibid, p. 321.
18. Ibid, p. 330.
19. Ibid, pp. 331–32.
20. Ibid, pp. 232–33. The original French is more modest and historically exact: 'Tandis que l'on édite de moins en moins d'ouvrages en latin, et une proportion toujours plus grande de textes en langue nationale, le commerce du livre se morcelle en Europe.' *L'Apparition du Livre*, p. 356.

populations, who, after all, are subjects, not citizens. In the modern conception, state sovereignty is fully, flatly, and evenly operative over each square centimetre of a legally demarcated territory. But in the older imagining, where states were defined by centres, borders were porous and indistinct, and sovereignties faded imperceptibly into one another.[21] Hence, paradoxically enough, the ease with which pre-modern empires and kingdoms were able to sustain their rule over immensely heterogeneous, and often not even contiguous, populations for long periods of time.[22]

One must also remember that these antique monarchical states expanded not only by warfare but by sexual politics – of a kind very different from that practised today. Through the general principle of verticality, dynastic marriages brought together diverse populations under new apices. Paradigmatic in this respect was the House of Habsburg. As the tag went, *Bella gerant alii tu felix Austria nube!* Here, in somewhat abbreviated form, is the later dynasts' titulature:[23]

> Emperor of Austria; King of Hungary, of Bohemia, of Dalmatia, Croatia, Slavonia, Galicia, Lodomeria, and Illyria; King of Jerusalem, etc.; Archduke of Austria [sic]; Grand Duke of Tuscany and Cracow; Duke of Loth [a] ringia, of Salzburg, Styria, Carinthia, Carniola, and Bukovina; Grand Duke of Transylvania, Margrave of Moravia; Duke of Upper and Lower Silesia, of Modena, Parma, Piacenza, and Guastella, of Ausschwitz and Sator, of Teschen, Friaul, Ragusa, and Zara; Princely Count of Habsburg and Tyrol, of Kyburg, Görz, and Gradiska; Duke of Trient and Brizen; Margrave of Upper and Lower Lausitz and in Istria; Count of Hohenembs, Feldkirch, Bregenz, Sonnenberg, etc.; Lord of Trieste, of Cattaro, and above the Windisch Mark; Great Voyvod of the Voyvodina, Servia. . . . etc.

This, Jászi justly observes, was, 'not without a certain comic aspect . . .

21. Notice the displacement in rulers' nomenclature that corresponds to this transformation. Schoolchildren remember monarchs by their first names (what *was* William the Conqueror's surname?), presidents by their last (what *was* Ebert's Christian name?). In a world of citizens, all of whom are theoretically eligible for the presidency, the limited pool of 'Christian' names makes them inadequate as specifying designators. In monarchies, however, where rule is reserved for a single surname, it is necessarily 'Christian' names, with numbers, or sobriquets, that supply the requisite distinctions.

22. We may here note in passing that Nairn is certainly correct in describing the 1707 Act of Union between England and Scotland as a 'patrician bargain,' in the sense that the union's architects were aristocratic politicians. (See his lucid discussion in *The Break-up of Britain*, pp. 136ff.) Still, it is difficult to imagine such a bargain being struck between the aristocracies of two republics. The conception of a United *Kingdom* was surely the crucial mediating element that made the deal possible.

23. Oscar Jászi, *The Dissolution of the Habsburg Monarchy*, p. 34.

the record of the innumerable marriages, hucksterings and captures of the Habsburgs.'

In realms where polygyny was religiously sanctioned, complex systems of tiered concubinage were essential to the integration of the realm. In fact, royal lineages often derived their prestige, aside from any aura of divinity, from, shall we say, miscegenation?[24] For such mixtures were signs of a superordinate status. It is characteristic that there has not been an 'English' dynasty ruling in London since the eleventh century (if then); and what 'nationality' are we to assign to the Bourbons?[25]

During the seventeenth century, however – for reasons that need not detain us here – the automatic legitimacy of sacral monarchy began its slow decline in Western Europe. In 1649, Charles Stuart was beheaded in the first of the modern world's revolutions, and during the 1650s one of the more important European states was ruled by a plebeian Protector rather than a king. Yet even in the age of Pope and Addison, Anne Stuart was still healing the sick by the laying on of royal hands, cures committed also by the Bourbons, Louis XV and XVI, in Enlightened France till the end of the *ancien régime*.[26] But after 1789 the principle of Legitimacy had to be loudly and self-consciously defended, and, in the process, 'monarchy' became a semi-standardized model. Tennō and Son of Heaven became 'Emperors'. In far-off Siam Rama V (Chulalongkorn) sent his sons and nephews to the courts of St. Petersburg, London, and Berlin to learn the intricacies of the world-model. In 1887, he instituted the requisite principle of succession-by-legal-primogeniture, thus bringing 'Siam into line with the "civilized" monarchies of Europe.'[27] The new system brought to the throne

24. Most notably in pre-modern Asia. But the same principle was at work in monogamous Christian Europe. In 1910, one Otto Forst put out his *Ahnentafel Seiner Kaiserlichen und Königlichen Hoheit des durchlauchtigsten Herrn Erzherzogs Franz Ferdinand*, listing 2,047 of the soon-to-be-assassinated Archduke's ancestors. The included 1,486 Germans, 124 French, 196 Italians, 89 Spaniards, 52 Poles, 47 Danes, 20 Englishmen/women, as well as four other nationalities. This 'curious document' is cited in ibid., p. 136, n. 1. I can not resist quoting here Franz Joseph's wonderful reaction to the news of his erratic heir-apparent's murder: 'In this manner a superior power has restored that order which I unfortunately was unable to maintain' (ibid., p. 125).

25. Gellner stresses the typical foreignness of dynasties, but interprets the phenomenon too narrowly: local aristocrats prefer an alien monarch because he will not take sides in their internal rivalries. *Thought and Change*, p. 136.

26. Marc Bloch, *Les Rois Thaumaturges*, pp. 390 and 398–99.

27. Noel A. Battye, 'The Military, Government and Society in Siam, 1868–1910,' PhD thesis, Cornell 1974, p. 270.

in 1910 an erratic homosexual who would certainly have been passed over in an earlier age. However, inter-monarchic approval of his ascension as Rama VI was sealed by the attendance at his coronation of princelings from Britain, Russia, Greece, Sweden, Denmark – and Japan![28]

As late as 1914, dynastic states made up the majority of the membership of the world political system, but, as we shall be noting in detail below, many dynasts had for some time been reaching for a 'national' cachet as the old principle of Legitimacy withered silently away. While the armies of Frederick the Great (r. 1740–1786) were heavily staffed by 'foreigners', those of his great-nephew Friedrich Wilhelm III (r. 1797–1840) were, as a result of Scharnhorst's, Gneisenau's and Clausewitz's spectacular reforms, exclusively 'national-Prussian.'[29]

Apprehensions of Time

It would be short-sighted, however, to think of the imagined communities of nations as simply growing out of and replacing religious communities and dynastic realms. Beneath the decline of sacred communities, languages and lineages, a fundamental change was taking place in modes of apprehending the world, which, more than anything else, made it possible to 'think' the nation.

To get a feeling for this change, one can profitably turn to the visual representations of the sacred communities, such as the reliefs and stained-glass windows of mediaeval churches, or the paintings of early Italian and Flemish masters. A characteristic feature of such representations is something misleadingly analogous to 'modern dress'. The shepherds who have followed the star to the manger where Christ is born bear the features of Burgundian peasants. The Virgin Mary is figured as a Tuscan merchant's daughter. In many paintings the commissioning patron, in full burgher or

28. Stephen Greene, 'Thai Government and Administration in the Reign of Rama VI (1910–1925),' PhD thesis, U. of London 1971, p. 92.

29. More than 1,000 of the 7,000–8,000 men on the Prussian Army's officer list in 1806 were foreigners. 'Middle-class Prussians were outnumbered by foreigners in their own army; this lent colour to the saying that Prussia was not a country that had an army, but an army that had a country.' In 1798, Prussian reformers had demanded a 'reduction by one half of the number of foreigners, who still amounted to about 50% of the privates. . . .' Alfred Vagts, *A History of Militarism*, pp. 64 and 85.

noble costume, appears kneeling in adoration alongside the shepherds. What seems incongruous today obviously appeared wholly natural to the eyes of mediaeval worshippers. We are faced with a world in which the figuring of imagined reality was overwhelmingly visual and aural. Christendom assumed its universal form through a myriad of specificities and particularities: this relief, that window, this sermon, that tale, this morality play, that relic. While the trans-European Latin-reading clerisy was one essential element in the structuring of the Christian imagination, the mediation of its conceptions to the illiterate masses, by visual and aural creations, always personal and particular, was no less vital. The humble parish priest, whose forebears and frailties everyone who heard his celebrations knew, was still the direct intermediary between his parishioners and the divine. This juxtaposition of the cosmic-universal and the mundane-particular meant that however vast Christendom might be, and was sensed to be, it manifested itself *variously* to particular Swabian or Andalusian communities as replications of themselves. Figuring the Virgin Mary with 'Semitic' features or 'first-century' costumes in the restoring spirit of the modern museum was unimaginable because the mediaeval Christian mind had no conception of history as an end-less chain of cause and effect or of radical separations between past and present.[30] Bloch observes that people thought they must be near the end of time, in the sense that Christ's second coming could occur at any moment: St. Paul had said that 'the day of the Lord cometh like a thief in the night.' It was thus natural for the great twelfth-century chronicler Bishop Otto of Freising to refer repeatedly to 'we who have been placed at the end of time.' Bloch concludes that as soon as mediaeval men 'gave themselves up to meditation, nothing was farther from their thoughts than the prospect of a long future for a young and vigorous human race.'[31]

Auerbach gives an unforgettable sketch of this form of consciousness:[32]

If an occurrence like the sacrifice of Isaac is interpreted as prefiguring the sacrifice of Christ, so that in the former the latter is as it were announced and promised and the latter 'fulfills' . . . the former, then a connection is estab-

30. For us, the idea of 'modern dress,' a metaphorical equivalencing of past with present, is a backhanded recognition of their fatal separation.

31. Bloch, *Feudal Society*, I, pp. 84–86.

32. Auerbach, *Mimesis*, p. 64. Emphasis added. Compare St. Augustine's description of the Old Testament as 'the shadow of [i.e. cast backwards by] the future.' Cited in Bloch, *Feudal Society*, I, p. 90.

lished between two events which are linked neither temporally nor causally – a connection which it is impossible to establish by reason in the horizontal dimension. . . . It can be established only if both occurrences are vertically linked to Divine Providence, which alone is able to devise such a plan of history and supply the key to its understanding . . . the here and now is no longer a mere link in an earthly chain of events, it is *simultaneously* something which has always been, and will be fulfilled in the future; and strictly, in the eyes of God, it is something eternal, something omnitemporal, something already consummated in the realm of fragmentary earthly event.

He rightly stresses that such an idea of *simultaneity* is wholly alien to our own. It views time as something close to what Benjamin calls Messianic time, a simultaneity of past and future in an instantaneous present.[33] In such a view of things, the word 'meanwhile' cannot be of real significance.

Our own conception of simultaneity has been a long time in the making, and its emergence is certainly connected, in ways that have yet to be well studied, with the development of the secular sciences. But it is a conception of such fundamental importance that, without taking it fully into account, we will find it difficult to probe the obscure genesis of nationalism. What has come to take the place of the mediaeval conception of simultaneity-along-time is, to borrow again from Benjamin, an idea of 'homogeneous, empty time,' in which simultaneity is, as it were, transverse, cross-time, marked not by prefiguring and fulfilment, but by temporal coincidence, and measured by clock and calendar.[34]

Why this transformation should be so important for the birth of the imagined community of the nation can best be seen if we consider the basic structure of two forms of imagining which first flowered in Europe in the eighteenth century: the novel and the newspaper.[35] For these forms provided the technical means for 're-presenting' the *kind* of imagined community that is the nation.

Consider first the structure of the old-fashioned novel, a structure typical not only of the masterpieces of Balzac but also of any contemporary dollar-dreadful. It is clearly a device for the presentation of simultaneity in

33. Walter Benjamin, *Illuminations*, p. 265.

34. Ibid., p. 263. So deep-lying is this new idea that one could argue that every essential modern conception is based on a conception of 'meanwhile'.

35. While the *Princesse de Clèves* had already appeared in 1678, the era of Richardson, Defoe and Fielding is the early eighteenth century. The origins of the modern newspaper lie in the Dutch gazettes of the late seventeenth century; but the newspaper only became a general category of printed matter after 1700. Febvre and Martin, *The Coming of the Book*, p. 197.

'homogeneous, empty time,' or a complex gloss upon the word 'mean-while'. Take, for illustrative purposes, a segment of a simple novel-plot, in which a man (A) has a wife (B) and a mistress (C), who in turn has a lover (D). We might imagine a sort of time-chart for this segment as follows:

Time:	I	II	III
Events:	A quarrels with B	A telephones C	D gets drunk in a bar
	C and D make love	B shops	A dines at home with B
		D plays pool	C has an ominous dream

Notice that during this sequence A and D never meet, indeed may not even be aware of each other's existence if C has played her cards right.[36] What then actually links A to D? Two complementary conceptions: First, that they are embedded in 'societies' (Wessex, Lübeck, Los Angeles). These societies are sociological entities of such firm and stable reality that their members (A and D) can even be described as passing each other on the street, without ever becoming acquainted, and still be connected.[37] Second, that A and D are embedded in the minds of the omniscient readers. Only they see the links. Only they, like God, watch A telephoning C, B shopping, and D playing pool all *at once.* That all these acts are performed at the same clocked, calendrical time, but by actors who may be largely unaware of one another, shows the novelty of this imagined world conjured up by the author in his readers' minds.[38]

The idea of a sociological organism moving calendrically through homogeneous, empty time is a precise analogue of the idea of the nation, which also is conceived as a solid community moving steadily down (or up) history.[39] An American will never meet, or even know the names of more than a handful of his 240,000,000-odd fellow-Americans. He has no idea of what they are up to at any one time. But he has complete confidence in their steady, anonymous, simultaneous activity.

36. Indeed, the plot's grip may *depend* at Times I, II, and III on A, B, C and D not knowing what the others are up to.

37. This polyphony decisively marks off the modern novel even from so brilliant a forerunner as Petronius's *Satyricon*. Its narrative proceeds single file. If Encolpius bewails his young lover's faithlessness, we are not simultaneously shown Gito in bed with Ascyltus.

38. In this context it is rewarding to compare any historical novel with documents or narratives from the period fictionalized.

39. Nothing better shows the immersion of the novel in homogeneous, empty time than the absence of those prefatory genealogies, often ascending to the origin of man, which are so characteristic a feature of ancient chronicles, legends, and holy books.

The perspective I am suggesting will perhaps seem less abstract if we turn to inspect briefly four fictions from different cultures and different epochs, all but one of which, nonetheless, are inextricably bound to nationalist movements. In 1887, the 'Father of Filipino Nationalism', José Rizal, wrote the novel *Noli Me Tangere*, which today is regarded as the greatest achievement of modern Filipino literature. It was also almost the first novel written by an 'Indio'.[40] Here is how it marvellously begins:[41]

> Don Santiago de los Santos was giving a dinner party one evening towards the end of October in the 1880's. Although, contrary to his usual practice, he had let it be known only on the afternoon of the same day, it was soon the topic of conversation in Binondo, where he lived, in other districts of Manila, and even in the Spanish walled city of Intramuros. Don Santiago was better known as Capitan Tiago — the rank was not military but political, and indicated that he had once been the native mayor of a town. In those days he had a reputation for lavishness. It was well known that his house, like his country, never closed its doors — except, of course, to trade and any idea that was new or daring.
>
> So the news of his dinner party ran like an electric shock through the community of spongers, hangers-on and gate-crashers whom God, in His infinite wisdom, had created and so fondly multiplied in Manila. Some of these set out to hunt polish for their boots; others, collar-buttons and cravats; but one and all gave the gravest thought to the manner in which they might greet their host with the assumed intimacy of long-standing friendship, or, if the occasion should arise, make a graceful apology for not having arrived earlier where presumably their presence was so eagerly awaited.
>
> The dinner was being given in a house on Anloague Street which may still be recognized unless it has tumbled down in some earthquake. Certainly it will not have been pulled down by its owner; in the Philippines, that is usually left to God and Nature. In fact, one often thinks that they are under contract to the Government for just that purpose. . . .

Extensive comment is surely unnecessary. It should suffice to note that right from the start the image (wholly new to Filipino writing) of a dinner-party being discussed by hundreds of unnamed people, who do not know each other, in quite different quarters of Manila, in a particular

40. Rizal wrote this novel in the colonial language (Spanish), which was then the lingua franca of the ethnically diverse Eurasian and native elites. Alongside the novel appeared also for the first time a 'nationalist' press, not only in Spanish but in such 'ethnic' languages as Tagalog and Ilocano. See Leopoldo Y. Yabes, 'The Modern Literature of the Philippines,' pp. 287–302, in Pierre-Bernard Lafont and Denys Lombard (eds), *Littératures Contemporaines de l'Asie du Sud-Est*.

41. José Rizal, *The Lost Eden, Noli Me Tangere*, p. 1.

month of a particular decade, immediately conjures up the imagined community. And in the phrase 'a house on Anloague Street which may still be recognized. . . .' the recognizers are we-the-Filipino-readers. The casual progression of this house from the 'interior' time of the novel to the 'exterior' time of the [Manila] reader's everyday life gives a hypnotic confirmation of the solidity of a single community, embracing characters, author and readers, moving onward through calendrical time. Notice too the tone. While Rizal has not the faintest idea of his readers' individual identities, he writes to them with an ironical intimacy, as though their relationships with each other are not to the smallest degree problematic.[42]

Nothing give one a more Foucaultian sense of abrupt discontinuities of consciousness than to compare *Noli* with the most celebrated previous literary work by an 'Indio', Francisco Baltazar's *Pinagdaanang Buhay ni Florante at ni Laura sa Cahariang Albania* [The Story of Florante and Laura in the Kingdom of Albania], the first printed edition of which dates from 1861, though it may have been composed as early as 1838.[43] For although Baltazar was still alive when Rizal was born, the world of his masterpiece is in every basic respect foreign to that of *Noli*. Its setting – a fabulous mediaeval Albania – is utterly removed in time and space from the Binondo of the 1880s. Its heroes – Florante, a Christian Albanian nobleman, and his bosom-friend Aladin, a Muslim ('Moro') Persian aristocrat – remind us of the Philippines only by the Christian-Moro linkage. Where Rizal deliberately sprinkles his Spanish prose with Tagalog words for 'realistic,' satirical, or nationalist effect, Baltazar unselfconsciously mixes Spanish phrases into his Tagalog quatrains simply to heighten the grandeur and sonority of his diction. *Noli* was meant to be read, while *Florante at Laura* was to be sung aloud. Most striking of all is Baltazar's handling of time. As Lumbera notes, 'the unravelling of the plot does not follow a chronological order. The story begins *in medias res*, so that the complete story comes to us through a series of speeches that serve as flashbacks.'[44] Almost half of the 399 quatrains are accounts of Florante's childhood, student years in

42. The obverse side of the readers' anonymous obscurity was/is the author's immediate celebrity. As we shall see, this obscurity/celebrity has everything to do with the spread of print-capitalism. As early as 1593 energetic Dominicans had published in Manila the *Doctrina Christiana*. But for centuries thereafter print remained under tight ecclesiastical control. Liberalization only began in the 1860s. See Bienvenido L. Lumbera, 'Tradition and Influences in the Development of Tagalog Poetry, 1570 to 1898', pp. 35, 143, and 236.

43. Ibid., pp. 173ff.

44. Ibid., pp. 205–6.

Athens, and subsequent military exploits, given by the hero in conversation with Aladin.[45] The 'spoken flashback' was for Baltazar the only alternative to a straightforward single-file narrative. If we learn of Florante's and Aladin's 'simultaneous' pasts, they are connected by their conversing voices, not by the structure of the epic. How distant this technique is from that of the novel: 'In that same spring, while Florante was still studying in Athens, Aladin was expelled from his sovereign's court . . .' In effect, it never occurs to Baltazar to 'situate' his protagonists in 'society,' or to discuss them with his audience. Nor, aside from the mellifluous flow of Tagalog polysyllables, is there much 'Filipino' about his text.[46]

In 1816, seventy years before the writing of *Noli*, José Joaquín Fernandez de Lizardi wrote a novel called *El Periquillo Sarniento* [The Itching Parrot], evidently the first Latin American work in this genre. In the words of one critic, this text is 'a ferocious indictment of Spanish administration in Mexico: ignorance, superstition and corruption are seen to be its most notable characteristics.'[47] The essential form of this 'nationalist' novel is indicated by the following description of its content:[48]

> From the first, [the hero, the Itching Parrot] is exposed to bad influences — ignorant maids inculcate superstitions, his mother indulges his whims, his teachers either have no vocation or no ability to discipline him. And though his father is an intelligent man who wants his son to practise a useful trade rather than swell the ranks of lawyers and parasites, it is Periquillo's over-fond mother who wins the day, sends her son to university and thus ensures that he will learn only superstitious nonsense . . . Periquillo remains incorrigibly ignorant despite many encounters with good and wise people. He is unwilling

45. The technique is similar to that of Homer, so ably discussed by Auerbach, *Mimesis*, ch. 1 ('Odysseus' Scar').

46. 'Paalam Albaniang pinamamayanan
ng casama, t, lupit, bangis caliluhan,
acong tangulan mo, i, cusa mang pinatay
sa iyo, i, malaqui ang panghihinayang.'
'Farewell, Albania, kingdom now
of evil, cruelty, brutishness and deceit!
I, your defender, whom you now murder
Nevertheless lament the fate that has befallen you.'
This famous stanza has sometimes been interpreted as a veiled statement of Filipino patriotism, but Lumbera convincingly shows such an interpretation to be an anachronistic gloss. 'Tradition and Influences,' pp. 214–15. The translation is Lumbera's. I have slightly altered his Tagalog text to conform to a 1973 edition of the poem based on the 1861 imprint.

47. Jean Franco, *An Introduction to Spanish-American Literature*, p. 34.

48. Ibid., pp. 35–36. Emphasis added.

to work or take anything seriously and becomes successively a priest, a gambler, a thief, apprentice to an apothecary, a doctor, clerk in a provincial town . . . These episodes *permit the author to describe hospitals, prisons, remote villages, monasteries*, while at the same time driving home one major point — that Spanish government and the education system encourage parasitism and laziness . . . Periquillo's adventures several times take him among Indians and Negroes . . .

Here again we see the 'national imagination' at work in the movement of a solitary hero through a sociological landscape of a fixity that fuses the world inside the novel with the world outside. This picaresque *tour d'horison* — hospital*s*, prison*s*, remote village*s*, monasterie*s*, Indian*s*, Negroe*s* — is nonetheless not a *tour du monde*. The horizon is clearly bounded: it is that of colonial Mexico. Nothing assures us of this sociological solidity more than the succession of plurals. For they conjure up a social space full of *comparable* prisons, none in itself of any unique importance, but all representative (in their simultaneous, separate existence) of the oppressiveness of *this* colony.[49] (Contrast prisons in the Bible. They are never imagined as *typical* of this or that society. Each, like the one where Salome was bewitched by John the Baptist, is magically alone.)

Finally, to remove the possibility that, since Rizal and Lizardi both wrote in Spanish, the frameworks we have been studying are somehow 'European,' here is the opening of *Semarang Hitam* [Black Semarang], a tale by the ill-fated young Indonesian communist-nationalist Mas Marco Kartodikromo,[50] published serially in 1924:[51]

> It was 7 o'clock, Saturday evening; young people in Semarang never stayed at home on Saturday night. On this night however nobody was about. Because the heavy day-long rain had made the roads wet and very slippery, all had stayed at home.
>
> For the workers in shops and offices Saturday morning was a time of anticipation — anticipating their leisure and the fun of walking around the city

49. This movement of a solitary hero through an adamantine social landscape is typical of many early (anti-)colonial novels.

50. After a brief, meteoric career as a radical journalist, Marco was interned by the Dutch colonial authorities in Boven Digul, one of the world's earliest concentration camps, deep in the interior swamps of western New Guinea. There he died in 1932, after six years confinement. Henri Chambert-Loir, 'Mas Marco Kartodikromo (c. 1890–1932) ou L'Education Politique,' p. 208, in *Littératures contemporaines de l'Asie du Sud-Est.*

51. As translated by Paul Tickell in his *Three Early Indonesian Short Stories by Mas Marco Kartodikromo (c. 1890–1932)*, p. 7. Emphasis added.

in the evening, but on this night they were to be disappointed — because of lethargy caused by the bad weather and the sticky roads in the kampungs. The main roads usually crammed with all sorts of traffic, the footpaths usually teeming with people, all were deserted. Now and then the crack of a horse-cab's whip could be heard spurring a horse on its way — or the clip-clop of horses' hooves pulling carriages along.

Semarang was deserted. The light from the rows of gas lamps shone straight down on the shining asphalt road. Occasionally the clear light from the gas lamps was dimmed as the wind blew from the east. . . .

A young man was seated on a long rattan lounge reading a newspaper. He was totally engrossed. His occasional anger and at other times smiles were a sure sign of his deep interest in the story. He turned the pages of the newspaper, thinking that perhaps he could find something that would stop him feeling so miserable. All of a sudden he came upon an article entitled:

PROSPERITY

A destitute vagrant became ill and died on the side of the road from exposure.

The young man was moved by this brief report. He could just imagine the suffering of the poor soul as he lay dying on the side of the road . . . One moment he felt an explosive anger well up inside. Another moment he felt pity. Yet another moment his anger was directed at the social system which gave rise to such poverty, while making a small group of people wealthy.

Here, as in *El Periquillo Sarniento*, we are in a world of plurals: shops, offices, carriages, kampungs, and gas lamps. As in the case of *Noli*, we-the-Indonesian-readers are plunged immediately into calendrical time and a familiar landscape; some of us may well have walked those 'sticky' Semarang roads. Once again, a solitary hero is juxtaposed to a socioscape described in careful, *general* detail. But there is also something new: a hero who is never named, but who is consistently referred to as '*our* young man'. Precisely the clumsiness and literary naivety of the text confirm the unself-conscious 'sincerity' of this pronominal adjective. Neither Marco nor his readers have any doubts about the reference. If in the jocular-sophisticated fiction of eighteenth- and nineteenth-century Europe the trope 'our hero' merely underlines an authorial play with a(ny) reader, Marco's 'our young man,' not least in its novelty, *means* a young man who belongs to the collective body of readers of *Indonesian*, and thus, implicitly, an embryonic Indonesian 'imagined community.' Notice that Marco feels no need to specify this community by name: it is already there. (Even if polylingual Dutch colonial censors could join his readership, they are excluded from this 'ourness,' as can be seen from the fact that the young man's anger is directed at 'the,' not 'our,' social system.)

Finally, the imagined community is confirmed by the doubleness of our reading about our young man reading. He does not find the corpse of the destitute vagrant by the side of a sticky Semarang road, but imagines it from the print in a newspaper.[52] Nor does he care the slightest who the dead vagrant individually was: he thinks of the representative body, not the personal life.

It is fitting that in *Semarang Hitam* a newspaper appears embedded in fiction, for, if we now turn to the newspaper as cultural product, we will be struck by its profound fictiveness. What is the essential literary convention of the newspaper? If we were to look at a sample front page of, say, *The New York Times*, we might find there stories about Soviet dissidents, famine in Mali, a gruesome murder, a coup in Iraq, the discovery of a rare fossil in Zimbabwe, and a speech by Mitterrand. Why are these events so juxtaposed? What connects them to each other? Not sheer caprice. Yet obviously most of them happen independently, without the actors being aware of each other or of what the others are up to. The arbitrariness of their inclusion and juxtaposition (a later edition will substitute a baseball triumph for Mitterrand) shows that the linkage between them is imagined.

This imagined linkage derives from two obliquely related sources. The first is simply calendrical coincidence. The date at the top of the newspaper, the single most important emblem on it, provides the essential connection – the steady onward clocking of homogeneous, empty time.[53] Within that time, 'the world' ambles sturdily ahead. The sign for this: if Mali disappears from the pages of *The New York Times* after two days of famine reportage, for months on end, readers do not for a moment imagine that Mali has disappeared or that famine has wiped out all its citizens. The novelistic format of the newspaper assures them that somewhere out there the 'character' Mali moves along quietly, awaiting its next reappearance in the plot.

52. In 1924, a close friend and political ally of Marco published a novel titled *Rasa Merdika* [Feeling Free/The Feel of Freedom]. Of the hero of this novel (which he wrongly atributes to Marco) Chambert-Loir writes that 'he has no idea of the meaning of the word "socialism": nonetheless he feels a profound malaise in the face of the social organization that surrounds him and he feels the need to enlarge his horizons by two methods: *travel and reading*.' ('Mas Marco', p. 208. Emphasis added.) The Itching Parrot has moved to Java and the twentieth century.

53. Reading a newspaper is like reading a novel whose author has abandoned any thought of a coherent plot.

The second source of imagined linkage lies in the relationship between the newspaper, as a form of book, and the market. It has been estimated that in the 40-odd years between the publication of the Gutenberg Bible and the close of the fifteenth century, more than 20,000,000 printed volumes were produced in Europe.[54] Between 1500 and 1600, the number manufactured had reached between 150,000,000 and 200,000,000.[55] 'From early on . . . the printing shops looked more like modern workshops than the monastic workrooms of the Middle Ages. In 1455, Fust and Schoeffer were already running a business geared to standardised production, and twenty years later large printing concerns were operating everywhere in all [sic] Europe.'[56] In a rather special sense, the book was the first modern-style mass-produced industrial commodity.[57] The sense I have in mind can be shewn if we compare the book to other early industrial products, such as textiles, bricks, or sugar. For these commodities are *measured* in mathematical amounts (pounds or loads or pieces). A pound of sugar is simply a quantity, a convenient load, not an object in itself. The book, however – and here it prefigures the durables of our time – is a distinct, self-contained object, exactly reproduced on a large scale.[58] One pound of sugar flows into the next; each book has its own eremitic self-sufficiency. (Small wonder that libraries, personal collections of mass-produced com-

54. Febvre and Martin, *The Coming of the Book*, p. 186. This amounted to no less than 35,000 editions produced in no fewer than 236 towns. As early as 1480, presses existed in more than 110 towns, of which 50 were in today's Italy, 30 in Germany, 9 in France, 8 each in Holland and Spain, 5 each in Belgium and Switzerland, 4 in England, 2 in Bohemia, and 1 in Poland. 'From that date it may be said of Europe that the printed book was in universal use.' (p. 182).

55. Ibid., p. 262. The authors comment that by the sixteenth century books were readily available to anyone who could read.

56. The great Antwerp publishing house of Plantin controlled, early in the sixteenth century, 24 presses with more than 100 workers in each shop. Ibid., p. 125.

57. This is one point solidly made amidst the vagaries of Marshall McLuhan's *Gutenberg Galaxy* (p. 125). One might add that if the book market was dwarfed by the markets in other commodities, its strategic role in the dissemination of ideas nonetheless made it of central importance to the development of modern Europe.

58. The principle here is more important than the scale. Until the nineteenth century, editions were still relatively small. Even Luther's Bible, an extraordinary best-seller, had only a 4,000-copy first edition. The unusually large first edition of Diderot's *Encyclopédie* numbered no more than 4,250. The average eighteenth-century run was less than 2,000. Febvre and Martin, *The Coming of the Book*, pp. 218–20. At the same time, the book was always distinguishable from other durables by its inherently limited market. Anyone with money can buy Czech cars; only Czech-readers will buy Czech-language books. The importance of this distinction will be considered below.

modities, were already a familiar sight, in urban centres like Paris, by the sixteenth century.)[59]

In this perspective, the newspaper is merely an 'extreme form' of the book, a book sold on a colossal scale, but of ephemeral popularity. Might we say: one-day best-sellers?[60] The obsolescence of the newspaper on the morrow of its printing – curious that one of the earlier mass-produced commodities should so prefigure the inbuilt obsolescence of modern durables – nonetheless, for just this reason, creates this extraordinary mass ceremony: the almost precisely simultaneous consumption ('imagining') of the newspaper-as-fiction. We know that particular morning and evening editions will overwhelmingly be consumed between this hour and that, only on this day, not that. (Contrast sugar, the use of which proceeds in an unclocked, continuous flow; it may go bad, but it does not go out of date.) The significance of this mass ceremony – Hegel observed that newspapers serve modern man as a substitute for morning prayers – is paradoxical. It is performed in silent privacy, in the lair of the skull.[61] Yet each communicant is well aware that the ceremony he performs is being replicated simultaneously by thousands (or millions) of others of whose existence he is confident, yet of whose identity he has not the slightest notion. Furthermore, this ceremony is incessantly repeated at daily or half-daily intervals throughout the calendar. What more vivid figure for the secular, historically-clocked, imagined community can be envisioned?[62] At the same time, the newspaper reader, observing exact replicas of his own paper being consumed by his subway, barbershop, or residential neighbours, is continually reassured that the imagined world is visibly rooted in everyday

59. Furthermore, as early as the late fifteenth century the Venetian publisher Aldus had pioneered the portable 'pocket edition.'

60. As the case of *Semarang Hitam* shows, the two kinds of best-sellers used to be more closely linked than they are today. Dickens too serialized his popular novels in popular newspapers.

61. 'Printed materials encouraged silent adherence to causes whose advocates could not be located in any one parish and who addressed an invisible public from afar.' Elizabeth L. Eisenstein, 'Some Conjectures about the Impact of Printing on Western Society and Thought,' *Journal of Modern History*, 40: 1 (March 1968), p. 42.

62. Writing of the relationship between the material anarchy of middle-class society and an abstract political state-order, Nairn observes that 'the representative mechanism converted real class inequality into the abstract egalitarianism of citizens, individual egotisms into an impersonal collective will, what would otherwise be chaos into a new state legitimacy.' *The Break-up of Britain*, p. 24. No doubt. But the representative mechanism (elections?) is a rare and moveable feast. The generation of the impersonal will is, I think, better sought in the diurnal regularities of the imagining life.

life. As with *Noli Me Tangere*, fiction seeps quietly and continuously into reality, creating that remarkable confidence of community in anonymity which is the hallmark of modern nations.

Before proceeding to a discussion of the specific origins of nationalism, it may be useful to recapitulate the main propositions put forward thus far. Essentially, I have been arguing that the very possibility of imagining the nation only arose historically when, and where, three fundamental cultural conceptions, all of great antiquity, lost their axiomatic grip on men's minds. The first of these was the idea that a particular script-language offered privileged access to ontological truth, precisely because it was an inseparable part of that truth. It was this idea that called into being the great transcontinental sodalities of Christendom, the Ummah Islam, and the rest. Second was the belief that society was naturally organized around and under high centres — monarchs who were persons apart from other human beings and who ruled by some form of cosmological (divine) dispensation. Human loyalties were necessarily hierarchical and centripetal because the ruler, like the sacred script, was a node of access to being and inherent in it. Third was a conception of temporality in which cosmology and history were indistinguishable, the origins of the world and of men essentially identical. Combined, these ideas rooted human lives firmly in the very nature of things, giving certain meaning to the everyday fatalities of existence (above all death, loss, and servitude) and offering, in various ways, redemption from them.

The slow, uneven decline of these interlinked certainties, first in Western Europe, later elsewhere, under the impact of economic change, 'discoveries' (social and scientific), and the development of increasingly rapid communications, drove a harsh wedge between cosmology and history. No surprise then that the search was on, so to speak, for a new way of linking fraternity, power and time meaningfully together. Nothing perhaps more precipitated this search, nor made it more fruitful, than print-capitalism, which made it possible for rapidly growing numbers of people to think about themselves, and to relate themselves to others, in profoundly new ways.

3
The Origins of
National Consciousness

If the development of print-as-commodity is the key to the generation of wholly new ideas of simultaneity, still, we are simply at the point where communities of the type 'horizontal-secular, transverse-time' become possible. Why, within that type, did the nation become so popular? The factors involved are obviously complex and various. But a strong case can be made for the primacy of capitalism.

As already noted, at least 20,000,000 books had already been printed by 1500,[1] signalling the onset of Benjamin's 'age of mechanical reproduction.' If manuscript knowledge was scarce and arcane lore, print knowledge lived by reproducibility and dissemination.[2] If, as Febvre and Martin believe, possibly as many as 200,000,000 volumes had been manufactured by 1600, it is no wonder that Francis Bacon believed that print had changed 'the appearance and state of the world.'[3]

One of the earlier forms of capitalist enterprise, book-publishing felt all of capitalism's restless search for markets. The early printers established branches all over Europe: 'in this way a veritable "international" of publishing houses, which ignored national [sic] frontiers, was created.'[4] And since the years 1500–1550 were a period of exceptional European prosperity, publishing shared in the general boom. 'More than at any other time' it was

1. The population of that Europe where print was then known was about 100,000,000. Febvre and Martin, *The Coming of the Book*, pp. 248–49.
2. Emblematic is Marco Polo's *Travels*, which remained largely unknown till its first printing in 1559. Polo, *Travels*, p. xiii.
3. Quoted in Eisenstein, 'Some Conjectures,' p. 56.
4. Febvre and Martin, *The Coming of the Book*, p. 122. (The original text, however, speaks simply of 'par-dessus les frontières.' *L'Apparition*, p. 184.)

'a great industry under the control of wealthy capitalists.'[5] Naturally, 'book-sellers were primarily concerned to make a profit and to sell their products, and consequently they sought out first and foremost those works which were of interest to the largest possible number of their contemporaries.'[6]

The initial market was literate Europe, a wide but thin stratum of Latin-readers. Saturation of this market took about 150 years. The determinative fact about Latin — aside from its sacrality — was that it was a language of bilinguals. Relatively few were born to speak it and even fewer, one imagines, dreamed in it. In the sixteenth century the proportion of bilinguals within the total population of Europe was quite small; very likely no larger than the proportion in the world's population today, and — proletarian internationalism notwithstanding — in the centuries to come. Then and now the vast bulk of mankind is monoglot. The logic of capitalism thus meant that once the elite Latin market was saturated, the potentially huge markets represented by the monoglot masses would beckon. To be sure, the Counter-Reformation encouraged a temporary resurgence of Latin-publishing, but by the mid-seventeenth century the movement was in decay, and fervently Catholic libraries replete. Meantime, a Europe-wide shortage of money made printers think more and more of peddling cheap editions in the vernaculars.[7]

The revolutionary vernacularizing thrust of capitalism was given further impetus by three extraneous factors, two of which contributed directly to the rise of national consciousness. The first, and ultimately the least important, was a change in the character of Latin itself. Thanks to the labours of the Humanists in reviving the broad literature of pre-Christian antiquity and spreading it through the print-market, a new appreciation of the sophisticated stylistic achievements of the ancients was apparent among the trans-European intelligentsia. The Latin they now aspired to write became more and more Ciceronian, and, by the same token, increasingly removed from ecclesiastical and everyday life. In this way it acquired an esoteric

5. Ibid., p. 187. The original text speaks of 'puissants' (powerful) rather than 'wealthy' capitalists. *L'Apparition*, p. 281.

6. 'Hence the introduction of printing was in this respect a stage on the road to our present society of mass consumption and of standardisation.' Ibid., pp. 259–60. (The original text has 'une civilisation de masse et de standardisation,' which may be better rendered 'standardised, mass civilization.' *L'Apparition*, p. 394).

7. Ibid., p. 195.

quality quite different from that of Church Latin in mediaeval times. For the older Latin was not arcane because of its subject matter or style, but simply because it was written at all, i.e. because of its status as *text*. Now it became arcane because of what was written, because of the language-in-itself.

Second was the impact of the Reformation, which, at the same time, owed much of its success to print-capitalism. Before the age of print, Rome easily won every war against heresy in Western Europe because it always had better internal lines of communication than its challengers. But when in 1517 Martin Luther nailed his theses to the chapel-door in Wittenberg, they were printed up in German translation, and 'within 15 days [had been] seen in every part of the country.'[8] In the two decades 1520–1540 three times as many books were published in German as in the period 1500–1520, an astonishing transformation to which Luther was absolutely central. His works represented no less than one third of *all* German-language books sold between 1518 and 1525. Between 1522 and 1546, a total of 430 editions (whole or partial) of his Biblical translations appeared. 'We have here for the first time a truly mass readership and a popular literature within everybody's reach.'[9] In effect, Luther became the first best-selling author *so known*. Or, to put it another way, the first writer who could 'sell' his *new* books on the basis of his name.[10]

Where Luther led, others quickly followed, opening the colossal religious propaganda war that raged across Europe for the next century. In this titanic 'battle for men's minds', Protestantism was always fundamentally on the offensive, precisely because it knew how to make use of the expanding vernacular print-market being created by capitalism, while the Counter-Reformation defended the citadel of Latin. The emblem for this is the Vatican's *Index Librorum Prohibitorum* – to which there was no Protestant counterpart – a novel catalogue made necessary by the sheer volume of printed subversion. Nothing gives a better sense of this siege mentality than François I's panicked 1535 ban on the printing of *any* books in his realm – on pain of death by hanging! The reason for both the ban and its

8. Ibid., pp. 289–90.
9. Ibid., pp. 291–95.
10. From this point it was only a step to the situation in seventeenth-century France where Corneille, Molière, and La Fontaine could sell their manuscript tragedies and comedies directly to publishers, who bought them as excellent investments in view of their authors' market reputations. Ibid., p. 161.

unenforceability was that by then his realm's eastern borders were ringed with Protestant states and cities producing a massive stream of smugglable print. To take Calvin's Geneva alone: between 1533 and 1540 only 42 editions were published there, but the numbers swelled to 527 between 1550 and 1564, by which latter date no less than 40 separate printing-presses were working overtime.[11]

The coalition between Protestantism and print-capitalism, exploiting cheap popular editions, quickly created large new reading publics — not least among merchants and women, who typically knew little or no Latin — and simultaneously mobilized them for politico-religious purposes. Inevitably, it was not merely the Church that was shaken to its core. The same earthquake produced Europe's first important non-dynastic, non-city states in the Dutch Republic and the Commonwealth of the Puritans. (François I's panic was as much political as religious.)

Third was the slow, geographically uneven, spread of particular vernaculars as instruments of administrative centralization by certain well-positioned would-be absolutist monarchs. Here it is useful to remember that the universality of Latin in mediaeval Western Europe never corresponded to a universal political system. The contrast with Imperial China, where the reach of the mandarinal bureaucracy and of painted characters largely coincided, is instructive. In effect, the political fragmentation of Western Europe after the collapse of the Western Empire meant that no sovereign could monopolize Latin and make it his-and-only-his language-of-state, and thus Latin's religious authority never had a true political analogue.

The birth of administrative vernaculars predated both print and the religious upheaval of the sixteenth century, and must therefore be regarded (at least initially) as an independent factor in the erosion of the sacred imagined community. At the same time, nothing suggests that any deep-seated ideological, let alone proto-national, impulses underlay this vernacularization where it occurred. The case of 'England' — on the northwestern periphery of Latin Europe — is here especially enlightening. Prior to the Norman Conquest, the language of the court, literary and administrative, was Anglo-Saxon. For the next century and a half virtually all royal documents were composed in Latin. Between about 1200 and 1350 this state-Latin was superseded by Norman French. In the meantime, a slow fusion

11. Ibid., pp. 310–15.

between this language of a foreign ruling class and the Anglo-Saxon of the subject population produced Early English. The fusion made it possible for the new language to take its turn, after 1362, as the language of the courts – and for the opening of Parliament. Wycliffe's vernacular *manuscript* Bible followed in 1382.[12] It is essential to bear in mind that this sequence was a series of 'state,' not 'national,' languages; and that the state concerned covered at various times not only today's England and Wales, but also portions of Ireland, Scotland *and France*. Obviously, huge elements of the subject populations knew little or nothing of Latin, Norman French, or Early English.[13] Not till almost a century *after* Early English's political enthronement was London's power swept out of 'France'.

On the Seine, a similar movement took place, if at a slower pace. As Bloch wrily puts it, 'French, that is to say a language which, since it was re-garded as merely a corrupt form of Latin, took several centuries to raise itself to literary dignity',[14] only became the official language of the courts of justice in 1539, when François I issued the Edict of Villers-Cotterêts.[15] In other dynastic realms Latin survived much longer – under the Habsburgs well into the nineteenth century. In still others, 'foreign' vernaculars took over: in the eighteenth century the languages of the Romanov court were French and German.[16]

In every instance, the 'choice' of language appears as a gradual, unself-conscious, pragmatic, not to say haphazard development. As such, it was utterly different from the self-conscious language policies pursued by nineteenth-century dynasts confronted with the rise of hostile popular linguistic-nationalisms. (See below, Chapter 6). One clear sign of the difference is that the old administrative languages were *just that*: languages used by and for officialdoms for their own inner convenience. There was no idea of systematically imposing the language on the dynasts' various sub-ject populations.[17] Nonetheless, the elevation of these vernaculars to the

---

12. Seton-Watson, *Nations and States*, pp. 28–29; Bloch, *Feudal Society*, I, p. 75.

13. We should not assume that administrative vernacular unification was immediately or fully achieved. It is unlikely that the Guyenne ruled from London was ever primarily adminis-tered in Early English.

14. Bloch, *Feudal Society*, I, p. 98.

15. Seton-Watson, *Nations and States*, p. 48.

16. Ibid., p. 83.

17. An agreeable confirmation of this point is provided by François I, who, as we have seen, banned all printing of books in 1535 and made French the language of his courts four years later!

status of languages-of-power, where, in one sense, they were competitors with Latin (French in Paris, [Early] English in London), made its own contribution to the decline of the imagined community of Christendom.

At bottom, it is likely that the esotericization of Latin, the Reformation, and the haphazard development of administrative vernaculars are significant, in the present context, primarily in a negative sense — in their contributions to the dethronement of Latin and the erosion of the sacred community of Christendom. It is quite possible to conceive of the emergence of the new imagined national communities without any one, perhaps all, of them being present. What, in a positive sense, made the new communities imaginable was a half-fortuitous, but explosive, interaction between a system of production and productive relations (capitalism), a technology of communications (print), and the fatality of human linguistic diversity.[18]

The element of fatality is essential. For whatever superhuman feats capitalism was capable of, it found in death and languages two tenacious adversaries.[19] Particular languages can die or be wiped out, but there was and is no possibility of man's general linguistic unification. Yet this mutual incomprehensibility was historically of only slight importance until capitalism and print created monoglot mass reading publics.

While it is essential to keep in mind an idea of fatality, in the sense of a *general* condition of irremediable linguistic diversity, it would be a mistake to equate this fatality with that common element in nationalist ideologies which stresses the primordial fatality of *particular* languages and their association with *particular* territorial units. The essential thing is the *interplay* between fatality, technology, and capitalism. In pre-print Europe, and, of course, elsewhere in the world, the diversity of spoken languages, those languages that for their speakers were (and are) the warp and woof of their lives, was immense; so immense, indeed, that had print-capitalism sought to exploit each potential oral vernacular market, it would have remained a capitalism of petty proportions. But these varied idiolects were capable of being assembled, within definite limits, into print-languages far fewer in

18. It was not the first 'accident' of its kind. Febvre and Martin note that while a visible bourgeoisie already existed in Europe by the late thirteenth century, paper did not come into general use until the end of the fourteenth. Only paper's smooth plane surface made the mass reproduction of texts and pictures possible — and this did not occur for still another seventy-five years. But paper was not a European invention. It floated in from another history — China's — through the Islamic world. *The Coming of the Book*, pp. 22, 30, and 45.

19. We still have no giant multinationals in the world of publishing.

number. The very arbitrariness of any system of signs for sounds facilitated the assembling process.[20] (At the same time, the more ideographic the signs, the vaster the potential assembling zone. One can detect a sort of descending hierarchy here from algebra through Chinese and English, to the regular syllabaries of French or Indonesian.) Nothing served to 'assemble' related vernaculars more than capitalism, which, within the limits imposed by grammars and syntaxes, created mechanically-reproduced print-languages, capable of dissemination through the market.[21]

These print-languages laid the bases for national consciousnesses in three distinct ways. First and foremost, they created unified fields of exchange and communications below Latin and above the spoken vernaculars. Speakers of the huge variety of Frenches, Englishes, or Spanishes, who might find it difficult or even impossible to understand one another in conversation, became capable of comprehending one another via print and paper. In the process, they gradually became aware of the hundreds of thousands, even millions, of people in their particular language-field, and at the same time that *only those* hundreds of thousands, or millions, so belonged. These fellow-readers, to whom they were connected through print, formed, in their secular, particular, visible invisibility, the embryo of the nationally-imagined community.

Second, print-capitalism gave a new fixity to language, which in the long run helped to build that image of antiquity so central to the subjective idea of the nation. As Febvre and Martin remind us, the printed book kept a permanent form, capable of virtually infinite reproduction, temporally and spatially. It was no longer subject to the individualizing and 'unconsciously modernizing' habits of monastic scribes. Thus, while twelfth-century French differed markedly from that written by Villon in the fifteenth, the rate of change slowed decisively in the sixteenth. 'By the 17th century

20. For a useful discussion of this point, see S. H. Steinberg, *Five Hundred Years of Printing*, chapter 5. That the sign *ough* is pronounced differently in the words although, bough, lough, rough, cough, and hiccough, shows both the idiolectic variety out of which the now-standard spelling of English emerged, and the ideographic quality of the final product.

21. I say 'nothing served . . . . more than capitalism' advisedly. Both Steinberg and Eisenstein come close to theomorphizing 'print' *qua* print as the genius of modern history. Febvre and Martin never forget that behind print stand printers and publishing firms. It is worth remembering in this context that although printing was invented first in China, possibly 500 years before its appearance in Europe, it had no major, let alone revolutionary impact – precisely because of the absence of capitalism there.

languages in Europe had generally assumed their modern forms.'[22] To put it another way, for now three centuries these stabilized print-languages have been gathering a darkening varnish; the words of our seventeenth-century forebears are accessible to us in a way that his twelfth-century ancestors were not to Villon.

Third, print-capitalism created languages-of-power of a kind different from the older administrative vernaculars. Certain dialects inevitably were 'closer' to each print-language and dominated their final forms. Their disadvantaged cousins, still assimilable to the emerging print-language, lost caste, above all because they were unsuccessful (or only relatively successful) in insisting on their own print-form. 'Northwestern German' became Platt Deutsch, a largely spoken, thus sub-standard German, because it was assimilable to print-German in a way that Bohemian spoken-Czech was not. High German, the King's English, and, later, Central Thai, were correspondingly elevated to a new politico-cultural eminence. (Hence the struggles in late-twentieth-century Europe for certain 'sub-'nationalities to change their subordinate status by breaking firmly into print – and radio.)

It remains only to emphasize that in their origins, the fixing of print-languages and the differentiation of status between them were largely unselfconscious processes resulting from the explosive interaction between capitalism, technology and human linguistic diversity. But as with so much else in the history of nationalism, once 'there,' they could become formal models to be imitated, and, where expedient, consciously exploited in a Machiavellian spirit. Today, the Thai government actively discourages attempts by foreign missionaries to provide its hill-tribe minorities with their own transcription-systems and to develop publications in their own languages: the same government is largely indifferent to what these minorities *speak*. The fate of the Turkic-speaking peoples in the zones incorporated into today's Turkey, Iran, Iraq, and the USSR is especially exemplary. A family of spoken languages, once everywhere assemblable, thus comprehensible, within an Arabic orthography, has lost that unity as a result of conscious manipulations. To heighten Turkish-Turkey's national consciousness at the expense of any wider Islamic identification, Atatürk

---

22. *The Coming of the Book*, p. 319. Cf. *L'Apparition*, p. 477: 'Au XVIIe siècle, les langues nationales apparaissent un peu partout cristallisées.'

imposed compulsory romanization.[23] The Soviet authorities followed suit, first with an anti-Islamic, anti-Persian compulsory romanization, then, in Stalin's 1930s, with a Russifying compulsory Cyrillicization.[24]

We can summarize the conclusions to be drawn from the argument thus far by saying that the convergence of capitalism and print technology on the fatal diversity of human language created the possibility of a new form of imagined community, which in its basic morphology set the stage for the modern nation. The potential stretch of these communities was inherently limited, and, at the same time, bore none but the most fortuitous relationship to existing political boundaries (which were, on the whole, the highwater marks of dynastic expansionisms).

Yet it is obvious that while today almost all modern self-conceived nations – and also nation-states – have 'national print-languages,' many of them have these languages in common, and in others only a tiny fraction of the population 'uses' the national language in conversation or on paper. The nation-states of Spanish America or those of the 'Anglo-Saxon family' are conspicuous examples of the first outcome; many ex-colonial states, particularly in Africa, of the second. In other words, the concrete formation of contemporary nation-states is by no means isomorphic with the determinate reach of particular print-languages. To account for the discontinuity-in-connectedness between print-languages, national consciousnesses, and nation-states, it is necessary to turn to the large cluster of new political entities that sprang up in the Western hemisphere between 1776 and 1838, all of which self-consciously defined themselves as nations, and, with the interesting exception of Brazil, as (non-dynastic) republics. For not only were they historically the first such states to emerge on the world stage, and therefore inevitably provided the first real models of what such states should 'look like,' but their numbers and contemporary births offer fruitful ground for comparative enquiry.

23. Hans Kohn, *The Age of Nationalism*, p. 108. It is probably only fair to add that Kemal also hoped thereby to align Turkish nationalism with the modern, romanized civilization of Western Europe.

24. Seton-Watson, *Nations and States*, p. 317.

4
Old Empires, New Nations

The new American states of the late eighteenth and early nineteenth centuries are of unusual interest because it seems almost impossible to explain them in terms of two factors which, probably because they are readily derivable from the mid-century nationalisms of Europe, have dominated much European thinking about the rise of nationalism.

In the first place, whether we think of Brazil, the USA, or the former colonies of Spain, language was not an element that differentiated them from their respective imperial metropoles. All, including the USA, were creole states, formed and led by people who shared a common language and common descent with those against whom they fought.[1] Indeed, it is fair to say that language was never even an issue in these early struggles for national liberation.

In the second place, there are serious reasons to doubt the applicability in much of the Western hemisphere of Nairn's otherwise persuasive thesis that:[2]

> The arrival of nationalism in a distinctively modern sense was tied to the political baptism of the lower classes. . . . Although sometimes hostile to democracy, nationalist movements have been invariably populist in outlook and sought to induct lower classes into political life. In its most typical version, this assumed the shape of a restless middle-class and intellectual leadership trying to stir up and channel popular class energies into support for the new states.

At least in South and Central America, European-style 'middle classes' were still insignificant at the end of the eighteenth century. Nor was there

---

1. Creole (*Criollo*) – person of (at least theoretically) pure European descent but born in the Americas (and, by later extension, anywhere outside Europe).
2. *The Break-up of Britain*, p. 41.

much in the way of an intelligentsia. For 'in those quiet colonial days little reading interrupted the stately and snobbish rhythm of men's lives.'[3] As we have seen, the first Spanish-American novel was only published in 1816, well after the wars for independence had broken out. The evidence clearly suggests that leadership was held by substantial landowners, allied with a much smaller number of merchants, and various types of professional (lawyers, military men, local and provincial functionaries).[4]

Far from seeking to 'induct the lower classes into political life,' one key factor initially spurring the drive for independence from Madrid, in such important cases as Venezuela, Mexico and Peru, was the *fear* of 'lower-class' political mobilizations: to wit, Indian or Negro-slave uprisings.[5] (This fear only increased when Hegel's 'secretary of the World-Spirit' conquered Spain in 1808, thereby depriving the creoles of peninsular military backup in case of emergency.) In Peru, memories of the great *jacquerie* led by Tupac Amarú (1740–1781) were still fresh.[6] In 1791, Toussaint L'Ouverture led an insurrection of black slaves that produced in 1804 the second independent republic in the Western hemisphere – and terrified the great slave-owning planters of Venezuela.[7] When, in 1789, Madrid issued a new, more humane, slave law specifying in detail the rights and duties of masters and slaves, 'the creoles rejected state intervention on the grounds that slaves were prone to vice and independence [!], and were essential to the economy. In Venezuela – indeed all over the Spanish Caribbean – planters resisted the law and procured its suspension in 1794.'[8] The Liberator Bolívar himself once opined that a Negro revolt was 'a thousand times worse than a Spanish invasion.'[9] Nor should we forget that many leaders of the independence movement in the Thirteen Colonies were slave-owning agrarian magnates. Thomas Jefferson himself was among the Virginian planters who in the 1770s were enraged by the loyalist governor's proclamation freeing those slaves who broke with their seditious

---

3. Gerhard Masur, *Simon Bolívar*, p. 17.

4. Lynch, *The Spanish-American Revolutions*, pp. 14–17 and passim. These proportions arose from the fact that the more important commercial and administrative functions were largely monopolized by Spain-born Spaniards, while land-owning was fully open to creoles.

5. In this respect there are clear analogies with Boer nationalism a century later.

6. It is perhaps notable that Tupac Amarú did not entirely repudiate allegiance to the Spanish king. He and his followers (largely Indians, but also some whites and mestizos) rose in fury against the regime in Lima: Masur, *Bolívar*, p. 24.

7. Seton-Watson, *Nations and States*, p. 201.

8. Lynch, *The Spanish-American Revolutions*, p. 192.

9. Ibid., p. 224.

masters.[10] It is instructive that one reason why Madrid made a successful come-back in Venezuela from 1814–1816 and held remote Quito until 1820 was that she won the support of slaves in the former, and of Indians in the latter, in the struggle against insurgent creoles.[11] Moreover, the long duration of the continental struggle against Spain, by then a second-rate European power and one itself recently conquered, suggests a certain 'social thinness' to these Latin American independence movements.

Yet they *were* national independence movements. Bolívar came to change his mind about slaves,[12] and his fellow-liberator San Martín decreed in 1821 that 'in the future the aborigines shall not be called Indians or natives; they are children *and citizens* of Peru and they shall be known as Peruvians.'[13] (We might add: in spite of the fact that as yet print-capitalism had not reached these illiterates.)

Here then is the riddle: why was it precisely *creole* communities that developed so early conceptions of their nation-ness — well before most of Europe? Why did such colonial provinces, usually containing large, oppressed, non-Spanish-speaking populations, produce creoles who consciously redefined these populations as fellow-nationals? And Spain,[14] to whom they were, in so many ways, attached, as an enemy alien? Why did the Spanish-American Empire, which had existed calmly for almost three centuries, quite suddenly fragment into eighteen separate states?

The two factors most commonly adduced in explanation are the tightening of Madrid's control and the spread of the liberalizing ideas of the Enlightenment in the latter half of the eighteenth century. It is undoubtedly true that the policies pursued by the capable 'enlightened despot'

10. Edward S. Morgan, 'The Heart of Jefferson,' *The New York Review of Books*, August 17, 1978, p. 2.

11. Masur, *Bolívar*, p. 207; Lynch, *The Spanish-American Revolutions*, p. 237.

12. Not without some twists and turns. He freed his own slaves shortly after Venezuela's declaration of independence in 1810. When he fled to Haiti in 1816, he obtained military assistance from President Alexandre Pétion in return for a promise to end slavery in all territories liberated. The promise was redeemed in Caracas in 1818 — but it should be remembered that Madrid's successes in Venezuela between 1814 and 1816 were in part due to *her* emancipation of loyal slaves. When Bolívar became president of Gran Colombia (Venezuela, New Granada and Ecuador) in 1821, he asked for and obtained from Congress a law freeing the *sons* of slaves. He 'had not asked Congress to wipe out slavery because he did not want to incur the resentment of the big landowners.' Masur, *Bolívar*, pp. 125, 206–207, 329, and 388.

13. Lynch, *The Spanish-American Revolutions*, p. 276. Emphasis added.

14. An anachronism. In the eighteenth century the usual term was still Las Españas [The Spains], not España [Spain]. Seton Watson, *Nations and States*, p. 53.

Carlos III (r. 1759–1788) increasingly frustrated, angered, and alarmed the upper creole classes. In what has sometimes sardonically been called the second conquest of the Americas, Madrid imposed new taxes, made their collection more efficient, enforced metropolitan commercial monopolies, restricted intra-hemispheric trade to its own advantage, centralized administrative hierarchies, and promoted a heavy immigration of *peninsulares*.[15] Mexico, for example, in the early eighteenth century provided the Crown with an annual revenue of about 3,000,000 pesos. By the century's end, however, the sum had almost quintupled, to 14,000,000, of which only 4,000,000 were used to defray the costs of local administration.[16] Parallel to this, the level of peninsular migration by the decade 1780–1790 was five times as high as it had been between 1710–1730.[17]

There is also no doubt that improving trans-Atlantic communications, and the fact that the various Americas shared languages and cultures with their respective metropoles, meant a relatively rapid and easy transmission of the new economic and political doctrines being produced in Western Europe. The success of the Thirteen Colonies' revolt at the end of the 1770s, and the onset of the French Revolution at the end of the 1780s, did not fail to exert a powerful influence. Nothing confirms this 'cultural revolution' more than the pervasive *republicanism* of the newly-independent communities.[18] Nowhere was any serious attempt made to recreate the dynastic principle in the Americas, except in Brazil; even there, it would probably not have been possible without the immigration in 1808 of the Portuguese dynast himself, in flight from Napoléon. (He stayed there for 13 years, and, on returning home, had his son crowned locally as Pedro I of Brazil.)

Yet the aggressiveness of Madrid and the spirit of liberalism, while central to any understanding of the impulse of resistance in the Spanish Americas, do not in themselves explain why entities like Chile, Venezuela, and Mexico turned out to be emotionally plausible and politically viable;[19]

15. This new metropolitan aggressiveness was partly the product of Enlightenment doctrines, partly of chronic fiscal problems, and partly, after 1779, of war with England. Lynch, *The Spanish-American Revolutions*, pp. 4–17.

16. Ibid., p. 301. Four million went to subsidize administration of other parts of Spanish America, while six millions were pure profit.

17. Ibid., p. 17.

18. The Constitution of the First Venezuelan Republic (1811) was in many places borrowed verbatim from that of the United States. Masur, *Bolívar*, p. 131.

19. Much the same could be said of London's stance vis-à-vis the Thirteen Colonies, and of the ideology of the 1776 Revolution.

nor why San Martín should decree that certain aborigines be identified by the neological 'Peruvians.' Nor, ultimately, do they account for the real sacrifices made. For while it is certain that the upper creole classes, *conceived as historical social formations*, did nicely out of independence over the long haul, many actual members of those classes *living* between 1808 and 1828 were financially ruined. (To take only one example: during Madrid's counter-offensive of 1814–16 'more than two-thirds of Venezuela's land-owning families suffered heavy confiscations.'[20]) And just as many willingly gave up their lives for the cause. This willingness to sacrifice on the part of comfortable classes is food for thought.

What then? The beginnings of an answer lie in the striking fact that 'each of the new South American republics had been an administrative unit from the sixteenth to the eighteenth century.'[21] In this respect they fore-shadowed the new states of Africa and parts of Asia in the mid-twentieth century, and form a sharp contrast to the new European states of the late nineteenth and early twentieth centuries. The original shaping of the American administrative units was to some extent arbitrary and fortuitous, marking the spatial limits of particular military conquests. But, over time, they developed a firmer reality under the influence of geographic, political and economic factors. The very vastness of the Spanish American empire, the enormous variety of its soils and climates, and, above all, the immense difficulty of communications in a pre-industrial age, tended to give these units a self-contained character. (In the colonial era the sea journey from Buenos Aires to Acapulco took four months, and the return trip even longer; the overland trek from Buenos Aires to Santiago normally lasted two months, and that to Cartagena nine.[22]) In addition, Madrid's com-mercial policies had the effect of turning administrative units into separate economic zones. 'All competition with the mother country was forbidden the Americans, and even the individual parts of the continent could not trade with each other. American goods en route from one side of America to the other had to travel circuitously through Spanish ports, and Spanish navigation had a monopoly on trade with the colonies.'[23] These experiences help to explain why 'one of the basic principles of the American revolution'

20. Lynch, *The Spanish-American Revolutions*, p. 208; cf. Masur, *Bolívar*, pp. 98–99 and 231.

21. Masur, *Bolívar*, p. 678.

22. Lynch, *The Spanish-American Revolutions*, pp. 25–26.

23. Masur, *Bolívar*, p. 19. Naturally these measures were only partially enforceable, and a good deal of smuggling always went on.

was that of '*uti possidetis* by which each nation was to preserve the territorial status quo of 1810, the year when the movement for independence had been inaugurated.'[24] Their influence also doubtless contributed to the break-up of Bolivar's short-lived Gran Colombía and of the United Provinces of the Rio de la Plata into their older constituents (which today are known as Venezuela-Colombia-Ecuador and Argentina-Uruguay-Paraguay-Bolivia). Nonetheless, *in themselves*, market-zones, 'natural'-geographic or politico-administrative, do not create attachments. Who will willingly die for Comecon or the EEC?

To see how administrative units could, over time, come to be conceived as fatherlands, not merely in the Americas but in other parts of the world, one has to look at the ways in which administrative organizations create meaning. The anthropologist Victor Turner has written illuminatingly about the 'journey', between times, statuses and places, as a meaning-creating experience.[25] All such journeys require interpretation (for example, the journey from birth to death has given rise to various religious conceptions.) For our purposes here, the modal journey is the pilgrimage. It is not simply that in the minds of Christians, Muslims or Hindus the cities of Rome, Mecca, or Benares were the centres of sacred geographies, but that their centrality was experienced and 'realized' (in the stagecraft sense) by the constant flow of pilgrims moving towards them from remote and *otherwise unrelated* localities. Indeed, in some sense the outer limits of the old religious communities of the imagination were determined by which pilgrimages people made.[26] As noted earlier, the strange physical juxtaposition of Malays, Persians, Indians, Berbers and Turks in Mecca is something incomprehensible without an idea of their community in some form. The Berber encountering the Malay before the Ka' bah must, as it were, ask himself: 'Why is this man doing what I am doing, uttering the same words that I am uttering, even though we can not talk to one another?' There is only one answer, once one has learnt it: 'Because *we* . . . are Muslims.' There was, to be sure, always a double aspect to the choreo-

24. Ibid., p. 546.
25. See his *The Forest of Symbols, Aspects of Ndembu Ritual*, especially the chapter 'Betwixt and Between: The Liminal Period in *Rites de Passage*.' For a later, more complex elaboration, see his *Dramas, Fields, and Metaphors, Symbolic Action in Human Society*, chapter 5 ('Pilgrimages as Social Processes') and 6 ('Passages, Margins, and Poverty: Religious Symbols of Communitas').
26. See Bloch, *Feudal Society*, I, p. 64.

graphy of the great religious pilgrimages: a vast horde of illiterate vernacular-speakers provided the dense, physical reality of the ceremonial passage; while a small segment of literate bilingual adepts drawn from each vernacular community performed the unifying rites, interpreting to their respective followings the meaning of their collective motion.[27] In a preprint age, the reality of the imagined religious community depended profoundly on countless, ceaseless travels. Nothing more impresses one about Western Christendom in its heyday than the uncoerced flow of faithful seekers from all over Europe, through the celebrated 'regional centres' of monastic learning, to Rome. These great Latin-speaking institutions drew together what today we would perhaps regard as Irishmen, Danes, Portuguese, Germans, and so forth, in communities whose sacred meaning was every day deciphered from their members' otherwise inexplicable juxtaposition in the refectory.

Though the religious pilgrimages are probably the most touching and grandiose journeys of the imagination, they had, and have, more modest and limited secular counterparts.[28] For our present purposes, the most important were the differing passages created by the rise of absolutizing monarchies, and, eventually, Europe-centred world-imperial states. The inner thrust of absolutism was to create a unified apparatus of power, controlled directly by, and loyal to, the ruler *over against* a decentralized, particularistic feudal nobility. Unification meant internal interchangeability of men and documents. Human interchangeability was fostered by the recruitment — naturally to varying extents — of *homines novi*, who, just for that reason, had no independent power of their own, and thus could serve as emanations of their masters' wills.[29] Absolutist functionaries thus undertook journeys which were basically different from those of feudal nobles.[30]

27. There are obvious analogies here with the respective roles of bilingual intelligentsias and largely illiterate workers and peasants in the genesis of certain nationalist movements — prior to the coming of radio. Invented only in 1895, radio made it possible to bypass print and summon into being an aural representation of the imagined community where the printed page scarcely penetrated. Its role in the Vietnamese and Indonesian revolutions, and generally in mid-twentieth-century nationalisms, has been much underestimated and understudied.

28. The 'secular pilgrimage' should not be taken merely as a fanciful trope. Conrad was being ironical, but also precise, when he described as 'pilgrims' the spectral agents of Leopold II in the heart of darkness.

29. Especially where: (a) monogamy was religiously and legally enforced; (b) primogeniture was the rule; (c) non-dynastic titles were both inheritable and conceptually and legally distinct from office-rank: i.e. where provincial aristocracies had significant independent power — England, as opposed to Siam.

30. See Bloch, *Feudal Society*, II, pp. 422ff.

The difference can be represented schematically as follows: In the modal feudal journey, the heir of Noble A, on his father's death, moves up one step to take that father's place. This ascension requires a round-trip, to the centre for investiture, and then back home to the ancestral demesne. For the new functionary, however, things are more complex. Talent, not death, charts his course. He sees before him a summit rather than a centre. He travels up its corniches in a series of looping arcs which, he hopes, will become smaller and tighter as he nears the top. Sent out to township A at rank V, he may return to the capital at rank W; proceed to province B at rank X; continue to vice-royalty C at rank Y; and end his pilgrimage in the capital at rank Z. On this journey there is no assured resting-place; every pause is provisional. The last thing the functionary wants is to return home; for he *has* no home with any intrinsic value. And this: on his upward-spiralling road he encounters as eager fellow-pilgrims his function-ary colleagues, from places and families he has scarcely heard of and surely hopes never to have to see. But in experiencing them as travelling-companions, a consciousness of connectedness ("Why are *we . . . here . . . together?*') emerges, above all when all share a single language-of-state. Then, if official A from province B administers province C, while official D from province C administers province B — a situation that absolutism begins to make likely — that experience of interchangeability requires its own explanation: the ideology of absolutism, which the new men them-selves, as much as the sovereign, elaborate.

Documentary interchangeability, which reinforced human inter-changeability, was fostered by the development of a standardized language-of-state. As the stately succession of Anglo-Saxon, Latin, Nor-man, and Early English in London from the eleventh through the four-teenth centuries demonstrates, *any* written language could, in principle, serve this function — provided it was given monopoly rights. (One could, however, argue that where vernaculars, rather than Latin, happened to hold the monopoly, a further centralizing function was achieved, by restricting the drift of one sovereign's officials to his rivals' machines: so to speak ensuring that Madrid's pilgrim-functionaries were not interchangeable with those of Paris.)

In principle, the extra-European expansion of the great kingdoms of early modern Europe should have simply extended the above model in the development of grand, transcontinental bureaucracies. But, in fact, this did not happen. The instrumental rationality of the absolutist apparatus —

above all its tendency to recruit and promote on the basis of talent rather than of birth – operated only fitfully beyond the eastern shores of the Atlantic.[31]

The pattern is plain in the Americas. For example, of the 170 viceroys in Spanish America prior to 1813, only 4 were creoles. These figures are all the more startling if we note that in 1800 less than 5% of the 3,200,000 creole 'whites' in the Western Empire (imposed on about 13,700,000 indigenes) were Spain-born Spaniards. On the eve of the revolution in Mexico, there was only one creole bishop, although creoles in the viceroy-alty outnumbered *peninsulares* by 70 to 1.[32] And, needless to say, it was nearly unheard-of for a creole to rise to a position of official importance in Spain.[33] Moreover, the pilgrimages of creole functionaries were not merely vertically barred. If peninsular officials could travel the road from Zaragoza to Cartagena, Madrid, Lima, and again Madrid, the 'Mexican' or 'Chilean' creole typically served only in the territories of colonial Mexico or Chile: his lateral movement was as cramped as his vertical ascent. In this way, the apex of his looping climb, the highest administrative centre to which he could be assigned, was the capital of the imperial administrative unit in which he found himself.[34] Yet on this cramped pilgrimage he found

31. Obviously this rationality should not be exaggerated. The case of the United King-dom, where Catholics were barred from office until 1829, is not unique. Can one doubt that this long exclusion played an important role in fostering Irish nationalism?

32. Lynch, *The Spanish-American Revolutions*, pp. 18–19, 298. Of the roughly 15,000 *peninsulares*, half were soldiers.

33. In the first decade of the nineteenth century there seem to have been about 400 South Americans resident in Spain at any one time. These included the 'Argentinian' San Martín, who was taken to Spain as a small boy, and spent the next 27 years there, entering the Royal Academy for noble youth, and playing a distinguished part in the armed struggle against Napoléon before returning to his homeland on hearing of its declaration of independence; and Bolívar, who for a time boarded in Madrid with Manuel Mello, 'American' lover of Queen Marie Louise. Masur describes him as belonging (c. 1805) to 'a group of young South Americans' who, like him, 'were rich, idle, and in disfavour with the Court. The hatred and sense of inferiority felt by many Creoles for the mother country was in them developing into revolutionary impulses.' *Bolívar*, pp. 41–47, and 469–70 (San Martín).

34. Over time, military pilgrimages became as important as civilian. 'Spain had neither the money nor the manpower to maintain large garrisons of regular troops in America, and she relied chiefly on colonial militias, which from the mid-eighteenth century were expanded and reorganized.' (Ibid., p. 10). These militias were quite local, not interchangeable parts of a continental security apparatus. They played an increasingly critical role from the 1760s on, as British incursions multiplied. Bolívar's father had been a prominent militia commander, defending Venezuelan ports against the intruders. Bolívar himself served in his father's old unit as a teenager. (Masur, *Bolívar*, pp. 30 and 38). In this respect he was typical of many of the first-generation nationalist leaders of Argentina, Venezuela, and Chile. See Robert L. Gilmore, *Caudillism and Militarism in Venezuela, 1810–1910*, chapter 6 ['The Militia'] and 7 ['The Military'].

travelling-companions, who came to sense that their fellowship was based not only on that pilgrimage's particular stretch, but on the shared fatality of trans-Atlantic birth. Even if he was born within one week of his father's migration, the accident of birth in the Americas consigned him to subordination – even though in terms of language, religion, ancestry, or manners he was largely indistinguishable from the Spain-born Spaniard. There was nothing to be done about it: he was *irremediably* a creole. Yet how irrational his exclusion must have seemed! Nonetheless, hidden inside the irrationality was this logic: born in the Americas, he could not be a true Spaniard; *ergo*, born in Spain, the *peninsular* could not be a true American.[35]

What made the exclusion appear rational in the metropole? Doubtless the confluence of a time-honoured Machiavellism with the growth of conceptions of biological and ecological contamination that accompanied the planetary spread of Europeans and European power from the sixteenth century onwards. From the sovereign's angle of vision, the American creoles, with their evergrowing numbers and increasing local rootedness with each succeeding generation, presented a historically unique political problem. For the first time the metropoles had to deal with – for that era – vast numbers of 'fellow-Europeans' (over three million in the Spanish Americas by 1800) far outside Europe. If the indigenes were conquerable by arms and disease, and controllable by the mysteries of Christianity and a completely alien culture (as well as, for those days, an advanced political organization), the same was not true of the creoles, who had virtually the same relationship to arms, disease, Christianity and European culture as the metropolitans. In other words, in principle, they had readily at hand the political, cultural and military means for successfully asserting themselves. They constituted simultaneously a colonial community and an upper class. They were to be economically subjected and exploited, but they were also essential to the stability of the empire. One can see, in this light, a certain parallelism between the position of the creole magnates and feudal barons, crucial to the sovereign's power, but also a menace to it. Thus the *peninsulares* dispatched as viceroys and bishops served the same

35. Notice the transformations that independence brought the Americans: first-generation immigrants now became 'lowest' rather than 'highest,' i.e. the ones most contaminated by a fatal place of birth. Similar inversions occur in response to racism. 'Black blood' – *taint* of the tar-brush – came, under imperialism, to be seen as hopelessly contaminating for any 'white.' Today, in the United States at least, the 'mulatto' has entered the museum. The tiniest trace of 'black blood' makes one beautifully Black. Contrast Fermín's optimistic program for miscegenation, and his absence of concern for the colour of the expected progeny.

functions as did the *homines novi* of the proto-absolutist bureaucracies.[36] Even if the viceroy was a grandee in his Andalusian home, here, 5,000 miles away, juxtaposed to the creoles, he was effectively a *homo novus* fully dependent on his metropolitan master. The tense balance between peninsular official and creole magnate was in this way an expression of the old policy of *divide et impera* in a new setting.

In addition, the growth of creole communities, mainly in the Americas, but also in parts of Asia and Africa, led inevitably to the appearance of Eurasians, Eurafricans, as well as Euramericans, not as occasional curiosities but as visible social groups. Their emergence permitted a style of thinking to flourish which foreshadows modern racism. Portugal, earliest of Europe's planetary conquerors, provides an apt illustration of this point. In the last decade of the fifteenth century Dom Manuel I could still 'solve' his 'Jewish question' by mass, forcible *conversion* – possibly the last European ruler to find this solution both satisfactory and 'natural'.[37] Less than a century later, however, one finds Alexandre Valignano, the great reorganizer of the Jesuit mission in Asia between 1574 and 1606, vehemently opposing the admission of Indians and Eurindians to the priesthood in these terms:[38]

> All these dusky races are very stupid and vicious, and of the basest spirits . . . As for the *mestiços* and *castiços*, we should receive either very few or none at all; especially with regard to the *mestiços*, since the more native blood they have, the more they resemble the Indians and the less they are esteemed by the Portuguese.

(Yet Valignano actively encouraged the admission of Japanese, Koreans, Chinese, and 'Indochinese' to the priestly function – perhaps because in those zones mestizos had yet to appear in any numbers?) Similarly, the Portuguese Franciscans in Goa violently opposed admission of creoles to the order, alleging that 'even if born of pure white parents [they] have been suckled by Indian ayahs in their infancy and thus had their blood contaminated for life.'[39] Boxer shows that 'racial' bars and exclusions increased markedly during the seventeenth and eighteenth centuries by comparison with earlier practice. To this malignant tendency the revival of large-scale

36. Given Madrid's deep concern that the management of the colonies be in trustworthy hands, 'it was axiomatic that the high posts be filled exclusively with native-born Spaniards'. Masur, *Bolívar*, p. 10.

37. Charles R. Boxer, *The Portuguese Seaborne Empire, 1415—1825*, p. 266.

38. Ibid., p. 252.

39. Ibid., p. 253.

slavery (for the first time in Europe since antiquity), which was pioneered by Portugal after 1510, made its own massive contribution. Already in the 1550s, 10% of Lisbon's population were slaves; by 1800 there were close to a million slaves among the 2,500,000 or so inhabitants of Portugal's Brazil.[40]

Indirectly, the Enlightenment also influenced the crystallization of a fatal distinction between metropolitans and creoles. In the course of his twenty-two years in power (1755–1777), the enlightened autocrat Pombal not only expelled the Jesuits from Portuguese domains, but made it a criminal offence to call 'coloured' subjects by offensive names, such as 'nigger' or 'mestiço' [sic]. But he justified this decree by citing ancient Roman conceptions of imperial citizenship, not the doctrines of the *philosophes*.[41] More typically, the writings of Rousseau and Herder, which argued that climate and 'ecology' had a constitutive impact on culture and character, exerted wide influence.[42] It was only too easy from there to make the convenient, vulgar deduction that creoles, born in a savage hemisphere, were by nature different from, and inferior to, the metropolitans – and thus unfitted for higher office.[43]

Our attention thus far has been focussed on the worlds of functionaries in the Americas – strategically important, but still small worlds. Moreover, they were worlds which, with their conflicts between *peninsulares* and creoles, predated the appearance of American national consciousnesses at the end of the eighteenth century. Cramped viceregal pilgrimages had no decisive consequences until their territorial stretch could be imagined as nations, in other words until the arrival of print-capitalism.

Print itself spread early to New Spain, but for two centuries it remained under the tight control of crown and church. Till the end of the seventeenth century, presses existed only in Mexico City and Lima, and their output was almost exclusively ecclesiastical. In Protestant North America printing scarcely existed at all in that century. In the course of the eigh-

---

40. Rona Fields, *The Portuguese Revolution and the Armed Forces Movement*, p. 15.

41. Boxer, *The Portuguese Seaborne Empire*, p. 257–58.

42. Kemiläinen, *Nationalism*, pp. 72–73.

43. I have emphasized here the racialist distinctions drawn between *peninsulares* and creoles because the main topic under review is the rise of creole nationalism. This should not be understood as minimizing the parallel growth of creole racism towards mestizos, Negroes, and Indians; nor the willingness of an unthreatened metropole to protect (up to a certain point) these unfortunates.

teenth, however, a virtual revolution took place. Between 1691 and 1820, no less than 2,120 'newspapers' were published, of which 461 lasted more than ten years.[44]

The figure of Benjamin Franklin is indelibly associated with creole nationalism in the northern Americas. But the importance of his trade may be less apparent. Once again, Febvre and Martin are enlightening. They remind us that 'printing did not really develop in [North] America during the eighteenth century until printers discovered a new source of income — the newspaper.'[45] Printers starting new presses always included a newspaper in their productions, to which they were usually the main, even the sole, contributor. Thus the printer-journalist was initially an essentially North American phenomenon. Since the main problem facing the printer-journalist was reaching readers, there developed an alliance with the postmaster so intimate that often each became the other. Hence, the printer's office emerged as the key to North American communications and community intellectual life. In Spanish America, albeit more slowly and intermittently, similar processes produced, in the second half of the eighteenth century, the first local presses.[46]

What were the characteristics of the first American newspapers, North or South? They began essentially as appendages of the market. Early gazettes contained — aside from news about the metropole — commercial news (when ships would arrive and depart, what prices were current for what commodities in what ports), as well as colonial political appointments, marriages of the wealthy, and so forth. In other words, what brought together, on the same page, *this* marriage with *that* ship, *this* price with *that* bishop, was the very structure of the colonial administration and market-system itself. In this way, the newspaper of Caracas quite naturally, and even apolitically, created an imagined community among a specific assemblage of fellow-readers, to whom *these* ships, brides, bishops, and prices belonged. In time, of course, it was only to be expected that political elements would enter in.

One fertile trait of such newspapers was always their provinciality. A colonial creole might read a Madrid newspaper if he got the chance (but it would say nothing about his world), but many a peninsular official, living down the same street, would, if he could help it, *not* read the Caracas

44. Febvre and Martin, *The Coming of the Book*, pp. 208–11.
45. Ibid., p. 211.
46. Franco, *An Introduction*, p. 28.

production. An asymmetry infinitely replicable in other colonial situations. Another such trait was plurality. The Spanish-American journals that developed towards the end of the eighteenth century were written in full awareness of provincials in worlds parallel to their own. The newspaper-readers of Mexico City, Buenos Aires, and Bogotá, even if they did not read each other's newspapers, were nonetheless quite conscious of their existence. Hence a well-known doubleness in early Spanish-American nationalism, its alternating grand stretch and particularistic localism. The fact that early Mexican nationalists wrote of themselves as *nosotros los Americanos* and of their country as *nuestra América*, has been interpreted as revealing the vanity of the local creoles who, because Mexico was far the most valuable of Spain's American possessions, saw themselves as the centre of the New World.[47] But, in fact, people all over Spanish America thought of themselves as 'Americans,' since this term denoted precisely the shared fatality of extra-Spanish birth.[48]

At the same time, we have seen that the very conception of the newspaper implies the refraction of even 'world events' into a specific imagined world of vernacular readers; and also how important to that imagined community is an idea of steady, solid simultaneity through time. Such a simultaneity the immense stretch of the Spanish American Empire, and the isolation of its component parts, made difficult to imagine.[49] Mexican creoles might learn months later of developments in Buenos Aires, but it would be through Mexican newspapers, not those of the Rio de la Plata; and the events would appear as 'similar to' rather than 'part of' events in Mexico.

In this sense, the 'failure' of the Spanish-American experience to generate a permanent Spanish-America-wide nationalism reflects both the general level of development of capitalism and technology in the late eighteenth century and the 'local' backwardness of Spanish capitalism and technology in relation to the administrative stretch of the empire. (The world-historical era in which each nationalism is born probably has a significant

47. Lynch, *The Spanish-American Revolutions*, p. 33.

48. 'A peon came to complain that the Spanish overseer of his estancia had beaten him. San Martín was indignant, but it was a nationalist rather than socialist indignation. "What do you think? After three years of revolution, a *maturrango* [vulg., Peninsular Spaniard] dares to raise his hand against an American!"' Ibid., p. 87.

49. A spell-binding evocation of the remoteness and isolation of the Spanish-American populations is Márquez's picture of the fabulous Macondo in *One Hundred Years of Solitude*.

impact on its scope. Is Indian nationalism not inseparable from colonial administrative-market unification, after the Mutiny, by the most formidable and advanced of the imperial powers?)

The Protestant, English-speaking creoles to the north were much more favourably situated for realizing the idea of 'America' and indeed eventually succeeded in appropriating the everyday title of 'Americans'. The original Thirteen Colonies comprised an area smaller than Venezuela, and one third the size of Argentina.[50] Bunched geographically together, their market-centres in Boston, New York, and Philadelphia were readily accessible to one another, and their populations were relatively tightly linked by print as well as commerce. The 'United States' could gradually multiply in numbers over the next 183 years, as old and new populations moved westwards out of the old east coast core. Yet even in the case of the USA there are elements of comparative 'failure' or shrinkage — non-absorption of English-speaking Canada, Texas's decade of independent sovereignty (1835–46). Had a sizeable English-speaking community existed in California in the eighteenth century, is it not likely that an independent state would have arisen there to play Argentina to the Thirteen Colonies' Peru? Even in the USA, the affective bonds of nationalism were elastic enough, combined with the rapid expansion of the western frontier and the contradictions generated between the economies of North and South, to precipitate a war of secession *almost a century after the Declaration of Independence*; and this war today sharply reminds us of those that tore Venezuela and Ecuador off from Gran Colombía, and Uruguay and Paraguay from the United Provinces of the Rio de la Plata.[51]

By way of provisional conclusion, it may be appropriate to re-emphasize the limited and specific thrust of the argument so far. It is intended less to explain the socio-economic bases of anti-metropolitan resistance in the Western hemisphere between say, 1760 and 1830, than why the resistance

50 The total area of the Thirteen Colonies was 322,497 square miles. That of Venezuela was 352,143; of Argentina, 1,072,067; and of Spanish South America, 3,417,625 square miles.

51. Paraguay forms a case of exceptional interest. Thanks to the relatively benevolent dictatorship established there by the Jesuits early in the seventeenth century, the indigenes were better treated than elsewhere in Spanish America, and Guaraní achieved the status of print-language. The Crown's expulsion of the Jesuits from Spanish America in 1767 brought the territory into the Rio de la Plata, but very late in the day, and for little more than a generation. See Seton-Watson, *Nations and States*, pp. 200–201.

was conceived in plural, 'national' forms – rather than in others. The economic interests at stake are well-known and obviously of fundamental importance. Liberalism and the Enlightenment clearly had a powerful impact, above all in providing an arsenal of ideological criticisms of imperial and *anciens régimes*. What I am proposing is that neither economic interest, Liberalism, nor Enlightenment could, or did, create *in themselves* the *kind*, or shape, of imagined community to be defended from these regimes' depredations; to put it another way, none provided the framework of a new consciousness – the scarcely-seen periphery of its vision – as opposed to centre-field objects of its admiration or disgust.[52] In accomplishing *this* specific task, pilgrim creole functionaries and provincial creole printmen played the decisive historic role.

52. It is instructive that the Declaration of Independence in 1776 speaks only of 'the people,' while the word 'nation' makes its debut only in the Constitution of 1789. Kemiläinen, *Nationalism*, p. 105.

5
Old Languages, New Models

The close of the era of successful national liberation movements in the Americas coincided rather closely with the onset of the age of nationalism in Europe. If we consider the character of these newer nationalisms which, between 1820 and 1920, changed the face of the Old World, two striking features mark them off from their ancestors. First, in almost all of them 'national print-languages' were of central ideological and political importance, whereas Spanish and English were never issues in the revolutionary Americas. Second, all were able to work from visible models provided by their distant, and after the convulsions of the French Revolution, not so distant, predecessors. The 'nation' thus became something capable of being consciously aspired to from early on, rather than a slowly sharpening frame of vision. Indeed, as we shall see, the 'nation' proved an invention on which it was impossible to secure a patent. It became available for pirating by widely different, and sometimes unexpected, hands. In this chapter, therefore the analytical focus will be on print-language and piracy.

In blithe disregard of some obvious extra-European facts, the great Johann Gottfried von Herder (1744–1803) had declared, towards the end of the eighteenth century, that: 'Denn *jedes* Volk ist Volk; es hat *seine* National Bildung wie *seine* Sprache.'[1] This splendidly *eng*-European conception of nation-ness as linked to a private-property language had wide influence in nineteenth-century Europe and, more narrowly, on subsequent theorizing about the nature of nationalism. What were the origins of this dream? Most probably, they lay in the profound shrinkage of the European world in time and space that began already in the fourteenth century, and

---

1. Kemiläinen, *Nationalism*, p. 42. Emphases added.

was caused initially by the Humanists' excavations and later, paradoxically enough, by Europe's planetary expansion.

As Auerbach so well expresses it:[2]

> With the first dawn of humanism, there began to be a sense that the events of classical history and legend and also those of the Bible were not separated from the present simply by an extent of time but also by *completely different conditions of life*. Humanism with its program of renewal of antique forms of life and expression creates a historical perspective in depth such as no previous epoch known to us possessed: the humanists see antiquity in historical depth, and, against that background, the dark epochs of the intervening Middle Ages. . . . [This made impossible] re-establishing the autarchic life natural to antique culture or the historical naiveté of the twelfth and thirteenth centuries.

The growth of what might be called 'comparative history' led in time to the hitherto unheard-of conception of a 'modernity' explicitly juxtaposed to 'antiquity,' and by no means necessarily to the latter's advantage. The issue was fiercely joined in the 'Battle of Ancients and Moderns' which dominated French intellectual life in the last quarter of the seventeenth century.[3] To quote Auerbach again, 'Under Louis XIV the French had the courage to consider their own culture a valid model on a par with that of the ancients, and they imposed this view upon the rest of Europe.'[4]

In the course of the sixteenth century, Europe's 'discovery' of grandiose civilizations hitherto only dimly rumoured – in China, Japan, Southeast Asia, and the Indian subcontinent – or completely unknown – Aztec Mexico and Incan Peru – suggested an irremediable human pluralism. Most of these civilizations had developed quite separate from the known history of Europe, Christendom, Antiquity, indeed man: their genealogies lay outside of and were unassimilable to Eden. (Only homogenous, empty time would offer them accommodation.) The impact of the 'discoveries' can be gauged by the peculiar geographies of the imaginary polities of the age. More's *Utopia*, which appeared in 1516, purported to be the account of a sailor, encountered by the author in Antwerp, who had participated in

---

2. *Mimesis*, p. 282. Emphasis added.

3. The battle opened in 1689 when the 59-year old Charles Perrault published his poem *Siècle de Louis le Grand*, which argued that the arts and sciences had come to their full flowering in his own time and place.

4. *Mimesis*, p. 343. Notice that Auerbach says 'culture,' not 'language.' We should also be chary of attributing 'nation-ness' to 'their own.'

Amerigo Vespucci's 1497–1498 expedition to the Americas. Francis Bacon's *New Atlantis* (1626) was perhaps new above all because it was situated in the Pacific Ocean. Swift's magnificent Island of the Houyhnhnms (1726) came with a bogus map of its South Atlantic location. (The meaning of these settings may be clearer if one considers how unimaginable it would be to place Plato's Republic on any map, sham or real.) All these tongue-in-cheek utopias, 'modelled' on real discoveries, are depicted, not as lost Edens, but as *contemporary* societies. One could argue that they had to be, since they were composed as criticisms *of* contemporary societies, and the discoveries had ended the necessity for seeking models in a vanished antiquity.[5] In the wake of the utopians came the luminaries of the Enlightenment, Vico, Montesquieu, Voltaire, and Rousseau, who increasingly exploited a 'real' non-Europe for a barrage of subversive writings directed against current European social and political institutions. In effect, it became possible to think of Europe as only one among many civilizations, and not necessarily the Chosen or the best.[6]

In due course, discovery and conquest also caused a revolution in European ideas about language. From the earliest days, Portuguese, Dutch, and Spanish seamen, missionaries, merchants and soldiers had, for practical reasons — navigation, conversion, commerce and war — gathered word-lists of non-European languages to be assembled in simple lexicons. But it was only in the later eighteenth century that the scientific comparative study of languages really got under way. Out of the English conquest of Bengal came William Jones' pioneering investigations of Sanskrit (1786), which led to a growing realization that Indic civilization was far older than that of Greece of Judaea. Out of Napoléon's Egyptian expedition came Jean Champollion's deciphérment of hieroglyphics (1835), which pluralized that extra-European antiquity.[7] Advances in Semitics undermined the idea that Hebrew was either uniquely ancient or of divine provenance. Once again, genealogies were being conceived which could only be accommodated by homogeneous, empty time. 'Language became less of a continuity

---

5. Similarly, there is a nice contrast between the two famous Mongols of English drama. Marlowe's *Tamburlaine the Great* (1587–1588) describes a fabulous dynast dead since 1407. Dryden's *Aurangzeb* (1676) depicts a contemporary reigning Emperor (1658–1707).

6. So, as European imperialism smashed its insouciant way around the globe, other civilizations found themselves traumatically confronted by pluralisms which annihilated their sacred genealogies. The Middle Kingdom's marginalization to the Far East is emblematic of this process.

7. Hobsbawm, *The Age of Revolution*, p. 337.

between an outside power and the human speaker than an internal field created and accomplished by language users among themselves.'[8] Out of these discoveries came philology, with its studies of comparative grammar, classification of languages into families, and reconstructions by scientific reasoning of 'proto-languages' out of oblivion. As Hobsbawm rightly observes, here was 'the first science which regarded evolution as its very core.'[9]

From this point on the old sacred languages – Latin, Greek, and Hebrew – were forced to mingle on equal ontological footing with a motley plebeian crowd of vernacular rivals, in a movement which complemented their earlier demotion in the market-place by print-capitalism. If all languages now shared a common (intra-)mundane status, then all were in principle equally worthy of study and admiration. But by who? Logically, since now none belonged to God, by their new owners: each language's native speakers – and readers.

As Seton-Watson most usefully shows, the nineteenth century was, in Europe and its immediate peripheries, a golden age of vernacularizing lexicographers, grammarians, philologists, and litterateurs.[10] The energetic activities of these professional intellectuals were central to the shaping of nineteenth-century European nationalisms in complete contrast to the situation in the Americas between 1770 and 1830. Monolingual dictionaries were vast compendia of each language's print-treasury, portable (if sometimes barely so) from shop to school, office to residence. Bilingual dictionaries made visible an approaching egalitarianism among languages – whatever the political realities outside, within the covers of the Czech-German/German-Czech dictionary the paired languages had a common status. The visionary drudges who devoted years to their compilation were of necessity drawn to or nurtured by the great libraries of Europe, above all those of the universities. And much of their immediate clientele was no less inevitably university and pre-university students. Hobsbawm's dictum that 'the progress of schools and universities measures that of nationalism, just as schools and especially universities became its most conscious champ-

8. Edward Said, *Orientalism*, p. 136.

9. Hobsbawm, *The Age of Revolution*, p. 337.

10. 'Just because history of language is usually in our time kept so rigidly apart from conventional political, economic and social history, it has seemed to me desirable to bring it together with these, even at the cost of less expertise.' *Nations and States*, p. 11. In fact, one of the most valuable aspects of Seton-Watson's text is precisely his attention to language history – though one can disagree with the way he employs it.

ions,' is certainly correct for nineteenth-century Europe, if not for other times and places.[11]

One can thus trace this lexicographic revolution as one might the ascending roar in an arsenal alight, as each small explosion ignites others, till the final general blaze turns night into day.

By the middle of the eighteenth century, the prodigious labours of German, French and English scholars had not only made available in handy printed form virtually the entire extant corpus of the Greek classics, along with the necessary philological and lexicographic adjuncts, but in dozens of books were recreating a glittering, and firmly pagan, ancient Hellenic civilization. In the last quarter of the century, this 'past' became increasingly accessible to a small number of young Greek-speaking Christian intellectuals, most of whom had studied or travelled outside the confines of the Ottoman Empire.[12] Exalted by the philhellenism at the centres of Western European civilization, they undertook the 'debarbarizing' of the modern Greeks, i.e., their transformation into beings worthy of Pericles and Socrates.[13] Emblematic of this change in consciousness are the following words of one of these young men, Adamantios Koraes (who later became an ardent lexicographer!), in an address to a French audience in Paris in 1803:[14]

> For the first time the nation surveys the hideous spectacle of its ignorance and trembles in measuring with the eye the distance separating it from its ancestors' glory. This painful *discovery*, however, does not precipitate the Greeks into despair: We are the descendants of Greeks, they implicitly told themselves, we must either try to become again worthy of this name, or we must not bear it.

11. *The Age of Revolution*, p. 166. Academic institutions were insignificant to the American nationalisms. Hobsbawm himself notes that though there were 6,000 students in Paris at the time, they played virtually no role in the French Revolution (p. 167). He also usefully reminds us that although education spread rapidly in the first half of the nineteenth century, the number of adolescents in schools was still minuscule by modern standards: a mere 19,000 *lycée* students in France in 1842; 20,000 high school pupils among the 68,000,000 population of Imperial Russia in 1850; a likely total of 48,000 university students in all Europe in 1848. Yet in the revolutions of *that* year, this tiny, but strategic, group played a pivotal role. (pp. 166–67).

12. The first Greek newspapers appeared in 1784 in Vienna. Philike Hetairia, the secret society largely responsible for the 1821 anti-Ottoman uprising, was founded in the 'great new Russian grain port of Odessa' in 1814.

13. See Elie Kedourie's introduction to *Nationalism in Asia and Africa*, p. 40.

14. Ibid., pp. 43–44. Emphasis added. The full text of Koraes's 'The Present State of Civilization in Greece' is given in pp. 157–82. It contains a stunningly modern analysis of the sociological bases for Greek nationalism.

Similarly in the late eighteenth century, grammars, dictionaries and histories of Rumanian appeared, accompanied by a drive, successful at first in the Habsburg realms, later in the Ottoman, for the replacement of Cyrillic by the Roman alphabet (marking Rumanian sharply off from its Slavic-Orthodox neighbours).[15] Between 1789 and 1794, the Russian Academy, modelled on the Academie Française, produced a six-volume Russian dictionary, followed by an official grammar in 1802. Both represented a triumph of the vernacular over Church Slavonic. Although right into the eighteenth century Czech was the language only of the peasantry in Bohemia (the nobility and rising middle classes spoke German), the Catholic priest Josef Dobrovský (1753–1829) produced in 1792 his *Geschichte der böhmische Sprache und ältern Literatur*, the first systematic history of the Czech language and literature. In 1835–39 appeared Josef Jungmann's pioneering five-volume Czech-German dictionary.[16]

Of the birth of Hungarian nationalism Ignotus writes that it is an event 'recent enough to be dated: 1772, the year of publication of some unreadable works by the versatile Hungarian author György Bessenyei, then a resident in Vienna and serving in Maria Theresa's bodyguard. . . . Bessenyei's *magna opera* were meant to prove that the Hungarian language was suitable for the very highest literary genre.'[17] Further stimulus was provided by the extensive publications of Ferenc Kazinczy (1759–1831), 'the father of Hungarian literature,' and by the removal, in 1784, of what became the University of Budapest to that city from the small provincial town of Trnava. Its first political expression was the Latin-speaking Magyar nobility's hostile reaction in the 1780s to Emperor Joseph II's decision to replace Latin by German as the prime language of imperial administration.[18]

In the period 1800–1850, as the result of pioneering work by native

15. Not pretending to any expert knowledge of Central and Eastern Europe, I have relied heavily on Seton-Watson in the analysis that follows. On Rumanian, see *Nations and States*, p. 177.

16. Ibid., pp. 150–153.

17. Paul Ignotus, *Hungary*, p. 44. 'He did prove it, but his polemical drive was more convincing than the aesthetic value of the examples he produced.' It is perhaps worth noting that this passage occurs in a subsection entitled 'The Inventing of the Hungarian Nation,' which opens with this pregnant phrase: 'A nation is born when a few people decide that it should be.'

18. Seton-Watson, *Nations and States*, pp. 158–61. The reaction was violent enough to persuade his successor Leopold II (r. 1790–1792) to reinstate Latin. See also below, Chapter VI. It is instructive that Kazinczy sided politically with Joseph II on this issue. (Ignotus, *Hungary*, p. 48).

scholars, three distinct literary languages were formed in the northern Balkans: Slovene, Serbo-Croat, and Bulgarian. If, in the 1830s, 'Bulgarians' had been widely thought to be of the same nation as the Serbs and Croats, and had in fact shared in the Illyrian Movement, a separate Bulgarian national state was to come into existence by 1878. In the eighteenth century, Ukrainian (Little Russian) was contemptuously tolerated as a language of yokels. But in 1798 Ivan Kotlarevsky wrote his *Aeneid*, an enormously popular satirical poem on Ukrainian life. In 1804, the University of Kharkov was founded and rapidly became the centre for a boom in Ukrainian literature. In 1819 appeared the first Ukrainian grammar – only 17 years after the official Russian one. And in the 1830s followed the works of Taras Shevchenko, of whom Seton-Watson observes that 'the formation of an accepted Ukrainian literary language owes more to him than to any other individual. The use of this language was the decisive stage in the formation of an Ukrainian national consciousness.'[19] Shortly thereafter, in 1846, the first Ukrainian nationalist organization was founded in Kiev – by a historian!

In the eighteenth century the language-of-state in today's Finland was Swedish. After the territory's union with Czardom in 1809, the official language became Russian. But an 'awakening' interest in Finnish and the Finnish past, first expressed through texts written in Latin and Swedish in the later eighteenth century, by the 1820s was increasingly manifested in the vernacular.[20] The leaders of the burgeoning Finnish nationalist movement were 'persons whose profession largely consisted of the handling of language: writers, teachers, pastors, and lawyers. The study of folklore and the rediscovery and piecing together of popular epic poetry went together with the publication of grammars and dictionaries, and led to the appearance of periodicals which served to standardize Finnish literary [i.e. print-] language, on behalf of which stronger political demands could be advanced.'[21] In the case of Norway, which had long shared a written language with the Danes, though with a completely different pronunciation, nationalism emerged with Ivar Aasen's new Norwegian grammar (1848) and dictionary (1850), texts which responded to and stimulated demands for a specifically Norwegian print-language.

19. *Nations and States*, p. 187. Needless to say, Czarism gave these people short shrift. Shevchenko was broken in Siberia. The Habsburgs, however, gave some encouragement to Ukrainian nationalists in Galicia – to counterbalance the Poles.

20. Kemiläinen, *Nationalism*, pp. 208–15.

21. Seton-Watson, *Nations and States*, p. 72.

Elsewhere, in the latter portion of the nineteenth century, we find Afrikaner nationalism pioneered by Boer pastors and litterateurs, who in the 1870s were successful in making the local Dutch patois into a literary language and naming it something no longer European. Maronites and Copts, many of them products of Beirut's American College (founded in 1866) and the Jesuit College of St. Joseph (founded in 1875) were major contributors to the revival of classical Arabic and the spread of Arab nationalism.[22] And the seeds of Turkish nationalism are easily detectable in the appearance of a lively vernacular press in Istanbul in the 1870s.[23]

Nor should we forget that the same epoch saw the vernacularization of another form of printed page: the score. After Dobrovský came Smetana, Dvořák, and Janáček; after Aasen, Grieg; after Kazinczy, Béla Bártok; and so on well into our century.

At the same time, it is self-evident that all these lexicographers, philologists, grammarians, folklorists, publicists, and composers did not carry on their revolutionary activities in a vacuum. They were, after all, producers for the print-market, and they were linked, via that silent bazaar, to consuming publics. Who were these consumers? In the most general sense: the families of the reading classes – not merely the 'working father,' but the servant-girded wife and the school-age children. If we note that as late as 1840, even in Britain and France, the most advanced states in Europe, almost half the population was still illiterate (and in backward Russia almost 98%), 'reading classes' meant people of some power. More concretely, they were, in addition to the old ruling classes of nobilities and landed gentries, courtiers and ecclesiastics, rising middle strata of plebeian lower officials, professionals, and commercial and industrial bourgeoisies.

Mid-nineteenth-century Europe witnessed a rapid increase in state expenditures and the size of state bureaucracies (civil and military), despite the absence of any major local wars. 'Between 1830 and 1850 public expenditure per capita increased by 25% in Spain, by 40% in France, by 44% in Russia, by 50% in Belgium, by 70% in Austria, by 75% in the U.S.A., and by over 90% in The Netherlands.'[24] Bureaucratic expansion,

22. Ibid., pp. 232 and 261.

23. Kohn, *The Age of Nationalism*, pp. 105–7. This meant rejection of 'Ottoman,' a dynastic officialese combining elements of Turkish, Persian, and Arabic. Characteristically, Ibrahim Sinasi, founder of the first such newspaper, had just returned from five years study in France. Where he led, others soon followed. By 1876, there were seven Turkish-language dailies in Constantinople.

24. Hobsbawm, *The Age of Revolution*, p. 229.

which also meant bureaucratic specialization, opened the gates of official preferment to much greater numbers and of far more varied social origins than hitherto. Take even the decrepit, sinecure-filled, nobility-ridden Austro-Hungarian state machinery: the percentage of men of middle class origins in the top echelons of its civil half rose from 0 in 1804, through 27 in 1829, 35 in 1859, to 55 in 1878. In the armed services, the same trend appeared, though characteristically at a slower, later pace: the middle class component of the officer corps rose from 10% to 75% between 1859 and 1918.[25]

If the expansion of bureaucratic middle classes was a relatively even phenomenon, occurring at comparable rates in both advanced and backward states of Europe, the rise of commercial and industrial bourgeoisies was of course highly uneven — massive and rapid in some places, slow and stunted in others. But no matter where, this 'rise' has to be understood in its relationship to vernacular print-capitalism.

The pre-bourgeois ruling classes generated their cohesions in some sense outside language, or at least outside print-language. If the ruler of Siam took a Malay noblewoman as a concubine, or if the King of England married a Spanish princess — did they ever talk seriously together? Solidarities were the products of kinship, clientship, and personal loyalties. 'French' nobles could assist 'English' kings against 'French' monarchs, not on the basis of shared language or culture, but, Machiavellian calculations aside, of shared kinsmen and friendships. The relatively small size of traditional aristocracies, their fixed political bases, and the personalization of political relations implied by sexual intercourse and inheritance, meant that their cohesions as classes were as much concrete as imagined. An illiterate nobility could still act as a nobility. But the bourgeoisie? Here was a class which, figuratively speaking, came into being as a class only in so many replications. Factory-owner in Lille was connected to factory-owner in Lyon only by reverberation. They had no necessary reason to know of one another's existence; they did not typically marry each other's daughters or inherit each other's property. But they did come to visualize in a general way the existence of thousands and thousands like themselves through print-language. For an illiterate bourgeoisie is scarcely imaginable. Thus in world-historical terms bourgeoisies were the first classes to achieve solidarities on an essentially imagined basis. But in a nineteenth-

25. Peter J. Katzenstein, *Disjoined Partners, Austria and Germany since 1815*, pp. 74, 112.

century Europe in which Latin had been defeated by vernacular print-capitalism for something like two centuries, these solidarities had an outermost stretch limited by vernacular legibilities. To put it another way, one can sleep with anyone, but one can only read some people's words.

Nobilities, landed gentries, professionals, functionaries, and men of the market – these then were the *potential* consumers of the philological revolution. But such a clientele was almost nowhere fully realized, and the combinations of actual consumers varied considerably from zone to zone. To see why, one has to return to the basic contrast drawn earlier between Europe and the Americas. In the Americas there was an almost perfect isomorphism between the stretch of the various empires and that of their vernaculars. In Europe, however, such coincidences were rare, and intra-European dynastic empires were basically polyvernacular. In other words, power and print-language mapped different realms.

The general growth in literacy, commerce, industry, communications and state machineries that marked the nineteenth century created powerful new impulses for vernacular linguistic unification within each dynastic realm. Latin hung on as a language-of-state in Austro-Hungary as late as the early 1840s, but it disappeared almost immediately thereafter. Language-of-state it might be, but it could not, in the nineteenth century, be the language of business, of the sciences, of the press, or of literature, especially in a world in which these languages continuously interpenetrated one another.

Meantime, vernacular languages-of-state assumed ever greater power and status in a process which, at least at the start, was largely unplanned. Thus English elbowed Gaelic out of most of Ireland, French pushed Breton to the wall, and Castilian reduced Catalan to marginality. In those realms, such as Britain and France, where, for quite extraneous reasons, there happened to be, by mid-century, a relatively high coincidence of language-of-state and language of the population,[26] the general interpenetration alluded to above did not have dramatic political effects. (These cases are closest to those of the Americas.) In many other realms, of which Austro-Hungary is probably the polar example, the consequences were inevitably explosive. In its huge, ramshackle, polyglot, but increasingly literate, domain the replacement of Latin by *any* vernacular, in the mid-nineteenth

26. As we have seen, vernacularization of the languages-of-state in these two realms was under way very early. In the case of the UK, the military subjugation of the Gaeltacht early in the eighteenth century and the Famine of the 1840s were powerful contributory factors.

century, promised enormous advantages to those of its subjects who *already* used that print-language, and appeared correspondingly menacing to those who did not. I emphasize the word *any*, since, as we shall be discussing in greater detail below, German's nineteenth century elevation by the Habsburg court, German as some might think it, had nothing whatever to do with German nationalism. (Under these circumstances, one would expect a self-conscious nationalism to arise *last* in each dynastic realm among the native-readers of the official vernacular. And such expectations are borne out by the historical record.)

In terms of our lexicographers' clienteles, it is therefore not surprising to find very different bodies of customers according to different political conditions. In Hungary, for example, where virtually no Magyar bourgeoisie existed, but 1 out of 8 claimed some aristocratic status, the parapets of print-Hungarian were defended against the German tide by segments of the petty nobility and an impoverished landed gentry.[27] Much the same could be said of Polish-readers. More typical, however, was a coalition of lesser gentries, academics, professionals, and businessmen, in which the first often provided leaders of 'standing,' the second and third myths, poetry, newspapers, and ideological formulations, and the last money and marketing facilities. The amiable Koraes offers us a fine vignette of the early clientele for Greek nationalism, in which intellectuals and entrepreneurs predominated:[28]

> In those towns which were less poor, which had some well-to-do inhabitants and a few schools, and therefore a few individuals who could at least read and understand the ancient writers, the revolution began earlier and could make more rapid and more comforting progress. In some of these towns, schools are already being enlarged, and the study of *foreign* languages and even of those sciences which are taught in Europe [sic] is being introduced into them. The wealthy sponsor the printing of books translated from Italian, French, German, and English; they send to Europe at their expense young men eager to learn; they give their children a better education, not excepting girls. . . .

---

27. Hobsbawm, *The Age of Revolution*, p. 165. For an excellent, detailed discussion, see Ignotus, *Hungary*, pp. 44–56; also Jászi, *The Dissolution*, pp. 224–25.

28. Kedourie, ed., *Nationalism in Asia and Africa*, p. 170. Emphasis added. Everything here is exemplary. If Koraes looks to 'Europe,' it is over his shoulder; he faces Constantinople. Ottoman is not yet a foreign language. And non-labouring future wives are entering the print-market.

Reading coalitions, with compositions that lay variously on the spectrum between Hungarian and Greek, developed similarly throughout Central and Eastern Europe, and into the Near East as the century proceeded.[29] How far the urban and rural masses shared in the new vernacularly-imagined communities naturally also varied a great deal. Much depended on the relationship between these masses and the missionaries of nationalism. At one extreme, perhaps, one might point to Ireland, where a Catholic priesthood drawn from the peasantry and close to it played a vital mediating role. Another extreme is suggested by Hobsbawm's ironic comment that: 'The Galician peasants in 1846 opposed the Polish revolutionaries even though these actually proclaimed the abolition of serfdom, preferring to massacre gentlemen and trust to the Emperor's officials.'[30] But everywhere, in fact, as literacy increased, it became easier to arouse popular support, with the masses discovering a new glory in the print elevation of languages they had humbly spoken all along.

Up to a point, then, Nairn's arresting formulation – 'The new middle-class intelligentsia of nationalism had to invite the masses into history; and the invitation-card had to be written in a language they understood'[31] – is correct. But it will be hard to see why the invitation came to seem so attractive, and why such different alliances were able to issue it (Nairn's middle-class intelligentsia was by no means the only host), unless we turn finally to piracy.

Hobsbawm observes that 'The French Revolution was not made or led by a formed party or movement in the modern sense, nor by men attempting to carry out a systematic programme. It hardly even threw up "leaders" of the kind to which twentieth century revolutions have accustomed us, until the post-revolutionary figure of Napoleon.'[32] But once it had occurred, it entered the accumulating memory of print. The overwhelming and bewildering concatenation of events experienced by its makers and its victims became a 'thing' – and with its own name: The French Revolution. Like a vast shapeless rock worn to a rounded boulder by countless drops of water, the experience was shaped by millions of printed words into a 'concept' on

29. For examples, see Seton-Watson, *Nations and States*, pp. 72 (Finland), 145 (Bulgaria), 153 (Bohemia), and 432 (Slovakia); Kohn, *The Age of Nationalism*, pp. 83 (Egypt) and 103 (Persia).
30. *The Age of Revolution*, p. 169.
31. *The Break-up of Britain*, p. 340.
32. *The Age of Revolution*, p. 80.

the printed page, and, in due course, into a model. Why 'it' broke out, what 'it' aimed for, why 'it' succeeded or failed, became subjects for endless polemics on the part of friends and foes: but of its 'it-ness', as it were, no one ever after had much doubt.[33]

In much the same way, the independence movements in the Americas became, as soon as they were printed about, 'concepts,' 'models,' and indeed 'blueprints.' In 'reality,' Bolívar's fear of Negro insurrections and San Martín's summoning of his indigenes to Peruvianness jostled one another chaotically. But printed words washed away the former almost at once, so that, if recalled at all, it appeared an inconsequential anomaly. Out of the American welter came these imagined realities: nation-states, republican institutions, common citizenships, popular sovereignty, national flags and anthems, etc., and the liquidation of their conceptual opposites: dynastic empires, monarchical institutions, absolutisms, sub-jecthoods, inherited nobilities, serfdoms, ghettoes, and so forth. (Nothing more stunning, in this context, than the general 'elision' of massive slavery from the 'modal' U.S.A. of the nineteenth century, and of the shared language of the 'modal' Southern republics.) Furthermore, the validity and generalizability of the blueprint were undoubtedly confirmed by the *plurality* of the independent states.

In effect, by the second decade of the nineteenth century, if not earlier, a 'model' of 'the' independent national state was available for pirating.[34] (The first groups to do so were the marginalized vernacular-based coalitions of the educated on which this chapter has been focussed.) But precisely because it was by then a known model, it imposed certain 'standards' from which too-marked deviations were impermissible. Even backward and reactionary Hungarian and Polish gentries were hard put to it not to make a show of 'inviting in' (if only to the pantry) their oppressed compatriots. If you like, the logic of San Martín's Peruvianization was at work. If 'Hungarians'

33. Compare: 'The very name of the Industrial Revolution reflects its relatively tardy impact on Europe. The thing [sic] existed in Britain before the word. Not until the 1820s did English and French socialists — themselves an unprecedented group — invent it, probably by analogy with the political revolution of France.' Ibid., p. 45.

34. It would be more precise, probably, to say that the model was a complex composite of French and American elements. But the 'observable reality' of France until after 1870 was restored monarchies and the ersatz dynasticism of Napoléon's great-nephew.

deserved a national state, then that *meant* Hungarians, all of them;[35] it meant a state in which the ultimate locus of sovereignty had to be the collectivity of Hungarian-speakers and readers; and, in due course, the liquidation of serfdom, the promotion of popular education, the expansion of the suffrage, and so on. Thus the 'populist' character of the early European nationalisms, even when led, demagogically, by the most backward social groups, was deeper than in the Americas: serfdom *had* to go, legal slavery was unimaginable – not least because the conceptual model was set in ineradicable place.

35. Not that this was a clear-cut matter. Half the subjects of the Kingdom of Hungary were non-Magyar. Only one third of the serfs were Magyar-speakers. In the early nineteenth century, the high Magyar aristocracy spoke French or German; the middle and lower nobility 'conversed in a dog-Latin strewn with Magyar, but also with Slovak, Serb, and Romanian expressions as well as vernacular German. . . .' Ignotus, *Hungary*, pp. 45–46, and 81.

6
Official Nationalism and Imperialism

In the course of the nineteenth century, and especially in its latter half, the philological-lexicographic revolution and the rise of intra-European nationalist movements, themselves the products, not only of capitalism, but of the elephantiasis of the dynastic states, created increasing cultural, and therefore political, difficulties for many dynasts. For, as we have seen, the fundamental legitimacy of most of these dynasties had nothing to do with nationalness. Romanovs ruled over Tatars and Letts, Germans and Armenians, Russians and Finns. Habsburgs were perched high over Magyars and Croats, Slovaks and Italians, Ukrainians and Austro-Germans. Hanoverians presided over Bengalis and Québecois, as well as Scots and Irish, English and Welsh.[1] On the continent, furthermore, members of the same dynastic families often ruled in different, sometimes rivalrous, states. What nationality should be assigned to Bourbons ruling in France and Spain, Hohenzollerns in Prussia and Rumania, Wittelsbachs in Bavaria and Greece?

We have also seen that for essentially administrative purposes these dynasties had, at different speeds, settled on certain print-vernaculars as languages-of-state – with the 'choice' of language essentially a matter of unselfconscious inheritance or convenience.

The lexicographic revolution in Europe, however, created, and gradually spread, the conviction that languages (in Europe at least) were, so to speak, the personal property of quite specific groups – their daily speakers and

---

1. It is nice that what eventually became the late British Empire has not been ruled by an 'English' dynasty since the early eleventh century: since then a motley parade of Normans (Plantagenets), Welsh (Tudors), Scots (Stuarts), Dutch (House of Orange) and Germans (Hanoverians) have squatted on the imperial throne. No one much cared till the philological revolution and a paroxysm of English nationalism in World War I. House of Windsor rhymes with House of Schönbrunn or House of Versailles.

readers – and moreover that these groups, imagined as communities, were entitled to their autonomous place in a fraternity of equals. The philological incendiaries thus presented the dynasts with a disagreeable dilemma which did not fail to sharpen over time. Nowhere is this dilemma clearer than in the case of Austro-Hungary. When the enlightened absolutist Joseph II decided early in the 1780s to switch the language of state from Latin to German, 'he did not fight, for instance, against the Magyar language, but he fought against the Latin . . . . He thought that, on the basis of the mediaeval Latin administration of the nobility, no effective work in the interest of the masses could have been carried on. The necessity of a unifying language connecting all parts of his empire seemed to him a peremptory claim. Under this necessity he could not choose any other language than German, the only one which had a vast culture and literature under its sway and which had a considerable minority in all his provinces.'[2] Indeed, 'the Habsburgs were *not* a consciously and consequentially Germanizing power . . . . There were *Habsburgs who did not even speak German*. Even those Habsburg emperors who sometimes fostered a policy of Germanization were not led in their efforts by any nationalistic point of view, but their measures were dictated by the intent of unification and universalism of their empire.'[3] Their essential aim was Hausmacht. After the middle of the nineteenth century, however, German increasingly acquired a double status: 'universal-imperial' and 'particular-national'. The more the dynasty pressed German in its first capacity, the more it appeared to be siding with its German-speaking subjects, and the more it aroused antipathy among the rest. Yet if it did not so press, indeed made concessions to other languages, above all Hungarian, not only was unification set back, but its German-speaking subjects allowed themselves to feel affronted. Thus it threatened to be hated simultaneously as champion of the Germans and traitor to them. (In much the same way, the Ottomans came to be hated by Turkish-speakers as apostates and by non-Turkish-speakers as Turkifiers.)

Insofar as all dynasts by mid-century were using *some* vernacular as language-of-state,[4] and also because of the rapidly rising prestige all over

2. Jászi, *The Dissolution*, p. 71. It is interesting that Joseph had refused to take the coronation oath as King of Hungary because this would have committed him to respecting the 'constitutional' privileges of the Magyar nobility. Ignotus, *Hungary*, p. 47.

3. Ibid., p. 137. Emphasis added.

4. One could argue that a long era closed in 1844, when Magyar finally replaced Latin as language-of-state in the Kingdom of Hungary. But, as we have seen, dog-Latin was in fact the *vernacular* of the Magyar middle and lower nobility until well into the nineteenth century.

Europe of the national idea, there was a discernible tendency among the Euro-Mediterranean monarchies to sidle towards a beckoning national identification. Romanovs discovered they were Great Russians, Hanoverians that they were English, Hohenzollerns that they were Germans – and with rather more difficulty their cousins turned Rumanian, Greek, and so forth. On the other hand, these new identifications shored up legitimacies which, in an age of capitalism, scepticism, and science, could less and less safely rest on putative sacrality and sheer antiquity. On the other hand, they also posed new dangers. If Kaiser Wilhelm II cast himself as 'No. I German,' he implicitly conceded that he was *one among many of the same kind as himself*, that he had a representative function, and therefore could, in principle, be a *traitor* to his fellow-Germans (something inconceivable in the dynasty's heyday. Traitor to whom or to what?) In the wake of the disaster that overtook Germany in 1918, he was taken at his implied word. Acting in the name of the German nation, civilian politicians (publicly) and the General Staff (with its usual courage, secretly) sent him packing from the Fatherland to an obscure Dutch suburb. So too Reza Pahlavi, having cast himself, not as Shah, but as Shah of Iran, came to be branded traitor. That he himself accepted, not the verdict, but, as it were, the jurisdiction of the national court, is shown by a small comedy at the moment of his departure into exile. Before climbing the ramp of his jet, he kissed the earth for the photographers and announced that he was taking a small quantity of sacred Iranian soil with him. This take is lifted from a film about Garibaldi, not the Sun King.

The 'naturalizations' of Europe's dynasties – maneuvers that required in many cases some diverting acrobatics – eventually led to what Seton-Watson bitingly calls 'official nationalisms,'[5] of which Czarist Russification is only the best-known example. These 'official nationalisms' can best be understood as a means for combining naturalization with retention of dynastic power, in particular over the huge polyglot domains accumulated since the Middle Ages; or, to put it another way, for stretching the short, tight, skin of the nation over the gigantic body of the empire. 'Russification' of the heterogeneous population of the Czar's subjects thus represented a violent, conscious welding of two opposing political orders, one

5. Seton-Watson, *Nations and States*, p. 148. Alas, the bite extends only to Eastern Europe. Seton-Watson is rightly sardonic at the expense of Romanov and Soviet regimes, but overlooks analogous policies being pursued in London, Paris, Berlin, Madrid and Washington.

ancient, one quite new. (While there is a certain analogy with, say, the Hispanization of the Americas and the Philippines, one central difference remains. The cultural conquistadors of late-nineteenth-century Czardom were proceeding from a selfconscious Machiavellism, while their sixteenth-century Spanish ancestors acted out of an unselfconscious everyday pragmatism. Nor was it for them really 'Hispanization' — rather it was simply *conversion* of heathens and savages.)

The key to situating 'official nationalism' — willed merger of nation and dynastic empire — is to remember that it developed *after*, and *in reaction to*, the popular national movements proliferating in Europe since the 1820s. If these nationalisms were modelled on American and French histories, so now they became modular in turn.[6] It was only that a certain inventive legerdemain was required to permit the empire to appear attractive in national drag.

To gain some perspective on this whole process of reactionary, secondary modelling, we may profitably consider some parallel, yet usefully contrasting cases.

How uneasy Romanov autocracy initially felt at 'taking to the streets' is excellently shown by Seton-Watson.[7] As noted earlier, the language of the court in St. Petersburg in the eighteenth century was French, while that of much of the provincial nobility was German. In the aftermath of Napoléon's invasion, Count Sergei Uvarov, in an official report of 1832, proposed that the realm should be based on the three principles of Autocracy, Orthodoxy, and Nationality (*natsionalnost*). If the first two were old, the third was quite novel — and somewhat premature in an age when half the 'nation' were still serfs, and more than half spoke a mother-tongue other than Russian. Uvarov's report won him the post of Minister of Education, but little more. For another half-century Czarism resisted Uvarovian enticements. It was not until the reign of Alexander III (1881–94) that Russification became official dynastic policy: long after Ukrainian, Finnish, Lett and other nationalisms had appeared within the Empire. Ironically enough, the first Russifying measures were taken against precisely those 'nationalities' which had been most *Kaisertreu* — such

6. There is an instructive parallel to all this in the politico-military reforms of Scharnhorst, Clausewitz and Gneisenau who in a self-consciously conservative spirit adapted many of the spontaneous innovations of the French Revolution for the erection of the great modular professionally-officered, standing, conscript army of the nineteenth century.

7. Ibid., pp. 83–87.

as the Baltic Germans. In 1887, Russian was made compulsory as the language of instruction in all state schools in the Baltic provinces above the lowest primary classes, a measure later extended to private schools as well. In 1893, the University of Dorpat, one of the most distinguished colleges in the imperial domains, was closed down because it used German in the lecture-rooms. (Recall that hitherto German had been a provincial language-of-state, *not* the voice of a popular nationalist movement). And so on. Seton-Watson even goes so far as to venture that the Revolution of 1905 was 'as much a revolution of non-Russians against Russification as it was a revolution of workers, peasants, and radical intellectuals against autocracy. The two revolts were of course connected: the social revolution was in fact most bitter in non-Russian regions, with Polish workers, Latvian peasants, and Georgian peasants as protagonists.'[8]

At the same time, it would be a big mistake to suppose that since Russification was a *dynastic* policy, it did not achieve one of its main purposes — marshalling a growing 'Great Russian' nationalism behind the throne. And not simply on the basis of sentiment. Enormous opportunities were after all available for Russian functionaries and entrepreneurs in the vast bureaucracy and expanding market that the empire provided.

No less interesting than Alexander III, Russifying Czar of All the Russias, is his contemporary Victoria von Saxe-Coburg-Gotha, Queen of England *and*, late in life, Empress of India. Actually her title is more interesting than her person, for it represents emblematically the thickened metal of a weld between nation and empire.[9] Her reign too marks the onset of a London-style 'official nationalism' which has strong affinities with the Russification being pursued in St. Petersburg. A good way to appreciate this affinity is by longitudinal comparison.

In *The Break-up of Britain*, Tom Nairn raises the problem of why there was no Scottish nationalist movement in the late eighteenth century, in spite of a rising Scots bourgeoisie and a very distinguished Scots intelligentsia.[10] Hobsbawm has peremptorily dismissed Nairn's thoughtful discussion with the remark: 'It is pure anachronism to expect [the Scots] to have demanded an independent state at this time.'[11] Yet if we

8. Ibid., p. 87.

9. This weld's disintegration is clocked by the procession from British Empire to British Commonwealth, to Commonwealth, to . . . .?

10. *The Break-up of Britain*, pp. 106ff.

11. 'Some Reflections,' p. 5.

recall that Benjamin Franklin, who co-signed the American Declaration of Independence, was born five years before David Hume, we may be inclined to think this judgment itself a shade anachronistic.[12] It seems to me that the difficulties – and their resolution – lie elsewhere.

On the other hand, there is Nairn's good nationalist tendency to treat his 'Scotland' as an unproblematic, primordial given. Bloch reminds us of the chequered ancestry of this 'entity', observing that the ravages of the Danes and William the Conqueror destroyed forever the cultural hegemony of Northern Anglo-Saxon Northumbria, symbolized by such luminaries as Alcuin and Bede:[13]

> A part of the northern zone was detached for ever from England proper. Cut off from other populations of Anglo-Saxon speech by the settlement of the Vikings in Yorkshire, the lowlands round about the Northumbrian citadel of Edinburgh fell under the domination of the Celtic chiefs of the hills. Thus the bilingual kingdom of Scotland was by a sort of backhanded stroke a creation of the Scandinavian invasions.

And Seton-Watson, for his part, writes that the Scottish language:[14]

> developed from the flowing together of Saxon and French, though with less of the latter, and with rather more from Celtic and Scandinavian sources than in the south. This language was spoken not only in the east of Scotland but also in northern England. Scots, or 'northern English,' was spoken at the Scottish court and by the social elite (who might or might not also speak Gaelic), as well as by the Lowland population as a whole. It was the language of the poets Robert Henryson and William Dunbar. It might have developed as a distinct literary language into modern times had not the union of the crowns in 1603 brought the predominance of southern English through its extension to the court, administration and upper class of Scotland.

The key point here is that already in the early seventeenth century large parts of what would one day be imagined as Scotland were English-speaking and had immediate access to print-English, provided a minimal degree of literacy existed. Then in the early eighteenth century the English-speaking Lowlands collaborated with London in largely exter-

---

12. In a book significantly entitled *Inventing America: Jefferson's Declaration of Independence*, Gary Wills argues in fact that the nationalist Jefferson's thinking was fundamentally shaped, not by Locke, but by Hume, Hutcheson, Adam Smith, and other eminences of the Scottish Enlightenment.

13. *Feudal Society*, I, p. 42.

14. *Nations and States*, pp. 30–31.

minating the Gaeltacht. In neither 'northward thrust' was a selfconscious Anglicizing policy pursued – in both cases Anglicization was essentially a byproduct. But combined, they had effectively eliminated, 'before' the age of nationalism, any possibility of a European-style vernacular-specific nationalist movement. Why not one in the American style? Part of the answer is given by Nairn in passing, when he speaks of a 'massive intellectual migration' southwards from the mid-eighteenth century onwards.[15] But there was more than an intellectual migration. Scottish politicians came south to legislate, and Scottish businessmen had open access to London's markets. In effect, in complete contrast to the Thirteen Colonies (and to a lesser extent Ireland), *there were no barricades* on all these pilgrims' paths towards the centre. (Compare the clear highway before Latin- and German-reading Hungarians to Vienna in the eighteenth century.) English had yet to become an 'English' language.

The same point can be made from a different angle. It is true that in the seventeenth century London resumed an acquisition of overseas territories arrested since the disastrous ending to the Hundred Years' War. But the 'spirit' of these conquests was still fundamentally that of a prenational age. Nothing more stunningly confirms this than the fact that 'India' only became 'British' twenty years after Victoria's accession to the throne. In other words, until after the 1857 Mutiny, 'India' was ruled by a commercial enterprise – not by a state, and certainly not by a nation-state.

But change was on the way. When the East India Company's charter came up for renewal in 1813, Parliament mandated the allocation of 100,000 rupees a year for the promotion of native education, *both* 'oriental' and 'Western.' In 1823, a Committee of Public Instruction was set up in Bengal; and in 1834, Thomas Babington Macaulay became president of this committee. Declaring that 'a single shelf of a good European library is worth the whole native literature of India and Arabia,'[16] he produced the following year his notorious 'Minute on Education'. Luckier than Uvarov, his recommendations went into immediate effect. A thoroughly English educational system was to be introduced which, in Macaulay's own ineffable words, would create 'a class of persons, Indian in blood and colour, but English in taste, in opinion, in morals and in intellect.'[17] In

15. *The Break-up of Britain*, p. 123.

16. We can be confident that this bumptious young middle-class English Uvarov knew nothing about either 'native literature'.

17. See Donald Eugene Smith, *India as a Secular State*, pp. 337–38; and Percival Spear, *India, Pakistan and the West*, p. 163.

1836, he wrote that:[18]

> No Hindu who has received an English education ever remains sincerely attached to his religion. It is my firm belief [so they always were] that if our plans of education are followed up, there will not be a single idolater among the respectable classes in Bengal thirty years hence.

There is here, to be sure, a certain naive optimism, which reminds us of Fermín in Bogotá half a century earlier. But the important thing is that we see a long-range (30 years!) policy, consciously formulated and pursued, to turn 'idolaters,' not so much into Christians, as into people culturally English, despite their irremediable colour and blood. A sort of mental miscegenation is intended, which, when compared with Fermín's physical one, shows that, like so much else in the Victorian age, imperialism made enormous progress in daintiness. In any event, it can be safely said that from this point on, all over the expanding empire, if at different speeds, Macaulayism was pursued.[19].

Like Russification, Anglicization naturally also offered rosy opportunities to armies of middle-class metropolitans (not least Scotsmen!) — functionaries, schoolmasters, merchants, and planters — who quickly fanned out over the vast, permanently sunlit realm. Nonetheless there was a central difference between the empires ruled from St. Petersburg and London. Czardom remained a 'continuous' continental domain, confined to the temperate and arctic zones of Eurasia. One could, so to speak, walk from one end of it to the other. Linguistic kinship with the Slavic populations of Eastern Europe, and — to put it pleasantly — historic political, religious and economic ties with many non-Slavic peoples, meant that *relatively* speaking, the barriers on the road to St. Petersburg were not impermeable.[20] The British Empire, on the other hand, was a grab-bag of primarily tropical possessions scattered over every continent. Only a minority of the subjected peoples had any long-standing religious, linguistic, cultural, even political and economic, ties with the metropole. Juxtaposed to one another in the Jubilee Year, they resembled those random collections of Old Mas-

18. Smith, *India*, p. 339.
19. See. for example, Roff's poker-faced account of the founding in 1905 of the Kuala Kangsar Malay College, which quickly became known, wholly without irony, as 'the Malay Eton.' True to Macaulay's prescriptions, its pupils were drawn from the 'respectable classes' — i.e. the compliant Malay aristocracy. Half the early boarders were direct descendants of various Malay sultans. William R. Roff, *The Origins of Malay Nationalism*, pp. 100–105.
20. The trans-Ural populations were another story.

ters hastily assembled by English and American millionaires which eventually turn into solemnly imperial state museums.

The consequences are well illustrated by the bitter recollections of Bipin Chandra Pal, who, a quarter of a century after India became independent, still felt angry enough to write that Indian Magistrates:[21]

> had not only passed a very rigid test on the same terms as British members of the service, but had spent the very best years of the formative period of their youth in England. Upon their return to their homeland, they practically lived in the same style as their brother Civilians, and *almost religiously* followed the social conventions and the ethical standards of the latter. In those days the India-born [sic – compare our Spanish-American creoles] Civilian practically cut himself off from his parent society, and lived and moved and had his being in the atmosphere so beloved of his British colleagues. *In mind and manners he was as much an Englishman as any Englishman.* It was no small sacrifice for him, because in this way he completely estranged himself from the society of his own people and became socially and morally a pariah among them . . . . He was as much a *stranger in his own native land* as the European residents in the country.

So far, so Macaulay. Much more serious, however, was that such strangers in their native land were *still* condemned – no less fatally than the American creoles – to an 'irrational' permanent subordination to the English maturrangos. It was not simply that, no matter how Anglicized a Pal became, he was always barred from the uppermost peaks of the Raj. He was also barred from movement outside its perimeters – laterally, say to the Gold Coast or Hong Kong, and vertically to the metropole. 'Completely estranged from the society of his own people' he might be, but he was under life sentence to serve among them. (To be sure, who 'they' included varied with the stretch of British conquests on the subcontinent.[22])

We shall be looking later at the consequences of official nationalisms for the rise of twentieth-century Asian and African nationalisms. For our purposes here, what needs to be stressed is that Anglicization produced thousands of Pals all over the world. Nothing more sharply underscores the fundamental contradiction of English official nationalism, i.e. the inner

21. See his *Memories of My Life and Times*, pp. 331–32. Emphases added.
22. It is true that Indian officials were employed in Burma; but Burma was administratively part of British India until 1937. Indians also served in subordinate capacities – especially in the police – in British Malaya and Singapore, but they served as 'locals' and 'immigrants,' i.e. were not transferable 'back' to India's police forces. Note that the emphasis here is on officials: Indian labourers, merchants, and even professionals, moved in sizeable numbers to South and East Africa, and even to the Caribbean.

incompatibility of empire and nation. I say 'nation' advisedly, because it is always tempting to account for these Pals in terms of racism. No one in their right mind would deny the profoundly racist character of nineteenth-century English imperialism. But the Pals also existed in the *white* colonies – Australia, New Zealand, Canada and South Africa. English and Scottish schoolmasters also swarmed there, and Anglicization was also cultural policy. And, as to Pal, to them the looping upward path still open to the Scots in the eighteenth century was closed. Anglicized Australians did not serve in Dublin or Manchester, and not even in Ottawa or Capetown. Nor, until quite late on, could they become Governors-General in Canberra.[23] Only 'English English' did, i.e. members of a half-concealed English nation.

Three years before the East India Company lost its Indian hunting-ground, Commodore Perry with his black ships peremptorily battered down the walls that for so long had kept Japan in self-imposed isolation. After 1854, the self-confidence and inner legitimacy of the Bakufu (Tokugawa Shogunate regime) were rapidly undermined by a conspicuous impotence in the face of the penetrating West. Under the banner of Sonnō Jōi (Revere the Sovereign, Expel the Barbarians), a small band of middle-ranking samurai, primarily from the Satsuma and Chōshū *han*, finally overthrew it in 1868. Among the reasons for their success was an exceptionally creative absorption, especially after 1860, of the new Western military science systematized since 1815 by Prussian and French staff professionals. They were thus able to make effective use of 7,300 ultra-modern rifles (most of them American Civil War scrap), purchased from an English arms-merchant.[24] 'In the use of guns . . . the men of Chōshū had such

23. To be sure, by late Edwardian times, a few 'white colonials' did migrate to London and became members of Parliament or prominent press-lords.
24. Here the key figure was Ōmura Masujirō (1824–1869), the so-called 'Father of the Japanese Army'. A low-ranking Chōshū samurai, he started his career by studying Western medicine through Dutch-language manuals. (It will be recalled that until 1854 the Dutch were the only Westerners permitted access to Japan, and this access was limited essentially to the island of Deshima off the Bakufu-controlled port of Nagasaki.) On graduating from the Tekijyuku in Osaka, then the best Dutch-language training centre in the country, he returned home to practise medicine – but without much success. In 1853, he took a position in Uwajima as instructor in Western learning, with a foray to Nagasaki to study naval science. (He designed and supervised the building of Japan's first steamship on the basis of written manuals.) His chance came after Perry's arrival; he moved to Edo in 1856 to work as an instructor at what would become the National Military Academy and at the Bakufu's top research office for the study of Western texts. His translations of European military works, especially on Napoleon's innovations in strategy and tactics, won him fame and recall to

mastery that the old blood and thunder slash and cut methods were quite useless against them.'[25]

Once in power, however, the rebels, whom we remember today as the Meiji oligarchs, found that their military prowess did not automatically guarantee political legitimacy. If the Tennō ('Emperor') could quickly be restored with the abolition of the Bakufu, the barbarians could not so easily be expelled.[26] Japan's geopolitical security remained just as fragile as before 1868. One of the basic means adopted for consolidating the oligarchy's domestic position was thus a variant of mid-century 'official nationalism,' rather consciously modelled on Hohenzollern Prussia-Germany. Between 1868 and 1871, all residual local 'feudal' military units were dissolved, giving Tokyo a centralized monopoly of the means of violence. In 1872, an Imperial Rescript ordered the promotion of universal literacy among adult males. In 1873, well before the United Kingdom, Japan introduced conscription. At the same time, the regime liquidated the samurai as a legally-defined and privileged class, an essential step not only for (slowly) opening the officer corps to all talents, but also to fit the now 'available' nation-of-citizens model. The Japanese peasantry was freed from subjection to the feudal *han*-system and henceforth exploited directly by the state and commercial-agricultural landowners.[27] In 1889, there followed a Prussian-style constitution and eventually universal male suffrage.

In this orderly campaign the men of Meiji were aided by three half-fortuitous factors. First was the relatively high degree of Japanese ethnocultural homogeneity resulting from two and a half centuries of isolation and internal pacification by the Bakufu. While the Japanese spoken in Kyūshū

Chōshū in 1860 to serve as military adviser. In 1864–65, he proved the relevance of his writings as a successful commander in the Chōshū civil war. Subsequently he became the first Meiji Minister of War, and drew up the regime's revolutionary plans for mass conscription and elimination of the samurai as a legal caste. For his pains he was assassinated by an outraged samurai. See Albert M. Craig, *Chōshū in the Meiji Restoration*, especially pp. 202–204, 267–280.

25. A contemporary Japanese observer, quoted in E. Herbert Norman, *Soldier and Peasant in Japan*, p. 31.

26. They knew this from bitter personal experience. In 1862, an English squadron had levelled half the Satsuma port of Kagoshima; in 1864, a joint American, Dutch, and English naval unit destroyed the Chōshū coastal fortifications at Shimonoseki. John M. Maki, *Japanese Militarism*, pp. 146–47.

27. All this reminds one of those reforms accomplished in Prussia after 1810 in response to Blücher's impassioned plea to Berlin: 'Get us a national army!' Vagts, *A History of Militarism*, p. 130; Cf. Gordon A. Craig, *The Politics of the Prussian Army*, ch. 2.

was largely incomprehensible in Honshū, and even Edo-Tokyo and Kyoto-Ōsaka found verbal communication problematic, the half-Sinified ideographic reading-system was long in place throughout the islands, and thus the development of mass literacy through schools and print was easy and uncontroversial. Second, the unique antiquity of the imperial house (Japan is the only country whose monarchy has been monopolized by a single dynasty throughout recorded history), and its indubitable Japanese-ness (contrast Bourbons and Habsburgs), made the exploitation of the Emperor for official-nationalist purposes rather simple. Third, the penetration of the barbarians was abrupt, massive, and menacing enough for most elements of the politically-aware population to rally behind a programme of self-defence conceived in the new national terms. It is worth emphasizing that this possibility had everything to do with the timing of Western penetration, i.e. the 1860s as opposed to the 1760s. For by then, in dominant Europe, the 'national community' had been coming into its own for half a century, in both popular and official versons. In effect, self-defence could be fashioned along lines and in accordance with what were coming to be 'international norms'.

That the gamble paid off, in spite of the terrible sufferings imposed on the peasantry by the ruthless fiscal exactions required to pay for a munitions-based programme of industrialization, was certainly due in part to the single-minded determination of the oligarchs themselves. Fortunate to come to power in an era in which numbered accounts in Zürich lay in an undreamed-of future, they were not tempted to move the exacted surplus outside Japan. Fortunate to rule in an age when military technology was still advancing at a relative amble, they were able, with their catch-up armaments programme, to turn Japan into an independent military power by the end of the century. Spectular successes by Japan's conscript army against China in 1894–5, and by her navy against Czardom in 1905, plus the annexation of Taiwan (1895) and Korea (1910), all consciously propagandized through schools and print, were extremely valuable in creating the general impression that the conservative oligarchy was an authentic representative of the nation of which Japanese were coming to imagine themselves members.

That this nationalism took on an aggressive imperialist character, even outside ruling circles, can best be accounted for by two factors: the legacy of Japan's long isolation and the power of the official-national model. Maruyama shrewdly points out that all nationalisms in Europe arose in the context of a traditional pluralism of interacting dynastic states – as I put it earlier, Latin's European universalism never had a political correlate:[28]

> National consciousness in Europe therefore bore from its inception the imprint of a consciousness of international society. It was a self-evident premise that disputes among sovereign states were conflicts among independent members of this international society. Precisely for this reason war, since Grotius, has come to occupy an important and systematic place in international law.

Centuries of Japanese isolation, however, meant that:[29]

> an awareness of equality in international affairs was totally absent. The advocates of expulsion [of the barbarians] viewed international relations from positions within the national hierarchy based on the supremacy of superiors over inferiors. Consequently, when the premises of the national hierarchy were transferred horizontally into the international sphere, international problems were reduced to a single alternative: conquer or be conquered. In the absence of any higher normative standards with which to gauge international relations, power politics is bound to be the rule and yesterday's timid defensiveness will become today's unrestrained expansionism.

Secondly, the oligarchy's prime models were the self-naturalizing dynasties of Europe. Insofar as these dynasties were more and more defining themselves in national terms, while at the same time expanding their power outside Europe, it is not surprising that the model should have been understood imperially.[30] As the parcellization of Africa at the Congress of Berlin (1885) showed, great nations were global conquerors. How plausible then to argue that for Japan to be accepted as 'great,' she too should turn Tennō into Emperor and launch overseas adventures, even if she was late to the game and had a lot of catching up to do. Few things give one a sharper sense of the way these residues impinged on the consciousness of the reading population than the following formulation by the radical-nationalist ideologue and revolutionary Kita Ikki (1884–1937), in his very influential *Nihon Kaizō Hōan Taikō* [Outline for the Reconstruction of Japan], published in 1924:[31]

> As the class struggle within a nation is waged for the readjustment of unequal distinctions, so war between nations for an honorable cause will reform the present unjust distinctions. The British Empire is a millionaire possessing

28. Maruyama Masao, *Thought and Behavior in Modern Japanese Politics*, p. 138.
29. Ibid., pp. 139–40.
30. Unluckily, the only alternative to the officially-nationalizing *dynastic* states of the time – Austro-Hungary – was not among the powers with a significant presence in the Far East.
31. As translated and cited in Richard Storry, *The Double Patriots*, p. 38.

wealth all over the world; and Russia is a great landowner in occupation of the northern half of the globe. Japan with her scattered fringe [sic] of islands is one of the proletariat, and she has the right to declare war on the big monopoly powers. The socialists of the West contradict themselves when they admit the right of class struggle to the proletariat at home and at the same time condemn war, waged by a proletariat among nations, as militarism and aggression . . . If it is permissible for the working class to unite to overthrow unjust authority by bloodshed, then unconditional approval should be given to Japan to perfect her army and navy and make war for the rectification of unjust international frontiers. In the name of rational social democracy Japan claims possession of Australia and Eastern Siberia.

It remains only to add that as the empire expanded after 1900, Japanification à la Macaulay was selfconsciously pursued as state policy. In the interwar years Koreans, Taiwanese and Manchurians, and, after the outbreak of the Pacific War, Burmese, Indonesians and Filipinos, were subjected to policies for which the European model was an established working practice. And just as in the British Empire, Japanified Koreans, Taiwanese or Burmese had their passages to the metropole absolutely barred. They might speak and read Japanese perfectly, but they would never preside over prefectures in Honshū, or even be posted outside their zones of origin.

Having considered these three varied cases of 'official nationalism', it is important to stress that the model could be selfconsciously followed by states with no serious great power pretensions, so long as they were states in which the ruling classes or leading elements in them felt threatened by the world-wide spread of the nationally-imagined community. A comparison between two such states, Siam and Hungary-within-Austro-Hungary, may prove instructive.

Meiji's contemporary, the long-reigning Chulalongkorn (r. 1868–1910), defended his realm from Western expansionism in a style that differed markedly from that of his Japanese opposite number.[32] Squeezed between British Burma and Malaya, and French Indochina, he devoted himself to a shrewd manipulative diplomacy rather than attempting to build up a serious war machine. (A Ministry of War was not established until 1894.) In a way that reminds one of eighteenth-century Europe, his armed forces were primarily a motley array of Vietnamese, Khmer, Lao, Malay, and Chinese mercenaries and tributaries. Nor was anything much done to push

32. The following section is a condensed version of part of my 'Studies of the Thai State: the State of Thai Studies', in Eliezer B. Ayal (ed.), *The State of Thai Studies*.

an official nationalism through a modernized educational system. Indeed, primary education was not made compulsory till more than a decade after his death, and the country's first university was not set up until 1917, four decades after the founding of the Imperial University in Tokyo. Nonetheless, Chulalongkorn regarded himself as a modernizer. But his prime models were not the United Kingdom or Germany, but rather the colonial *beamtenstaaten* of the Dutch East Indies, British Malaya, and the Raj.[33] Following these models meant rationalizing and centralizing royal government, eliminating traditional semi-autonomous tributary statelets, and promoting economic development somewhat along colonial lines. The most striking example of this – an example which in its odd way looks forward to contemporary Saudi Arabia – was his encouragement of a massive immigration of young, single, male foreigners to form a disoriented, politically powerless workforce needed to construct port facilities, build railway lines, dig canals, and expand commercial agriculture. This importing of *gastarbeiters* paralleled, indeed was modelled on, the policies of the authorities in Batavia and Singapore. And as in the case of the Netherlands Indies and British Malaya, the great bulk of the labourers imported during the nineteenth century were from southeastern China. It is instructive that this policy caused him neither personal qualms nor political difficulties – no more than it did the colonial rulers on whom he modelled himself. Indeed the policy made good short-term sense for a *dynastic* state, since it created an impotent working class 'outside' Thai society and left that society largely 'undisturbed'.

Wachirawut, his son and successor (r. 1910–1925), had to pick up the pieces, modelling himself this time on the self-naturalizing dynasts of Europe. Although – and because – he was educated in late Victorian England, he dramatized himself as his country's 'first nationalist.'[34] The target of this nationalism, however, was neither the United Kingdom, which controlled 90% of Siam's trade, nor France, which had recently made off with easterly segments of the old realm: it was the Chinese whom

33. Battye nicely shows that the purpose of the young monarch's visits to Batavia and Singapore in 1870 and to India in 1872 was, in Chulalongkorn's own sweet words, 'selecting what may be safe models.' See 'The Military, Government and Society in Siam, 1868–1910,' p. 118.

34. 'The inspiration of Vajiravudh's [Wachirawut's] nationalist program was, first and foremost, Great Britain, the Western nation Vajiravudh knew best, at this time a nation caught up in imperialist enthusiasm.' Walter F. Vella, *Chaiyo! King Vajiravudh and the Development of Thai Nationalism*, p. xiv. See also pp. 6 and 67–68.

his father had so recently and blithely imported. The style of his anti-Chinese stance is suggested by the titles of two of his most famous pamphlets: *The Jews of the Orient* (1914), and *Clogs on Our Wheels* (1915).

Why the change? Doubtless dramatic events immediately preceding and following his coronation in November 1910 had their effect. The previous June the police had had to be called out to suppress a general strike by Bangkok's Chinese merchants (upwardly mobile children of early immigrants) and workers, marking their initiation into Siamese politics.[35] The following year, the Celestial Monarchy in Peking was swept away by a heterogeneous assortment of groups from which merchants were by no means absent. 'The Chinese' thus appeared as harbingers of a populat *republicanism* profoundly threatening to the dynastic principle. Second, as the words 'Jews' and 'Orient' suggest, the Anglicized monarch had imbibed the particular racisms of the English ruling class. But, in addition, there was the fact that Wachirawut was a sort of Asian Bourbon. In a pre-national era his ancestors had readily taken attractive Chinese girls as wives and concubines, with the result that, Mendelianly-speaking, he himself had more Chinese 'blood' than Thai.[36]

Here is a fine example of the character of official nationalism – an anticipatory strategy adopted by dominant groups who are threatened with marginalization or exclusion from an emerging nationally-imagined community. (It goes without saying that Wachirawut also began moving all the policy levers of official nationalism: compulsory state-controlled primary education, state-organized propaganda, official rewriting of history, militarism – here more visible show than the real thing – and endless affirmations of the identity of dynasty and nation.[37])

The development of Hungarian nationalism in the nineteenth century shows in a different way the imprint of the 'official' model. We noted earlier the Latin-speaking Magyar nobility's enraged opposition to Joseph II's attempt in the 1780s to make German the sole imperial language-of-

35. The strike was occasioned by the government's decision to exact the same head-tax on the Chinese as the native Thai. Hitherto it had been lower, as an inducement to immigration. See Bevars D. Mabry, *The Development of Labor Institutions in Thailand*, p. 38. (Exploitation of the Chinese came mainly via the opium-farm.)

36. For genealogical details, see my 'Studies of the Thai State,' p. 214.

37. He also coined the slogan *Chat, Sasana, Kasat* (Nation, Religion, Monarch) which has been the shibboleth of rightwing regimes in Siam for the last quarter of a century. Here Uvarov's Autocracy, Orthodoxy, Nationality appear in reversed Thai order.

state. The more advantaged segments of this class feared losing their sine-cures under a centralized, streamlined administration dominated by imperial-German bureaucrats. The lower echelons were panicked by the possibility of losing their exemptions from taxes and compulsory military service, as well as their control over the serfs and rural counties. Yet alongside the defence of Latin, Magyar was, quite opportunistically, spoken for, 'since in the long run a Magyar administration seemed the only workable alternative to a German one.'[38] Béla Grünwald sardonically noted that 'the same counties which (arguing against the decree of the Emperor) emphasized the possibility of an administration in the Magyar tongue, declared it in 1811 – that is, twenty-seven years later – an impossibility.' Two decades later still, in a very 'nationalistic' Hungarian county it was said that 'the introduction of the Magyar language would endanger our constitution and all our interests.'[39] It was really only in the 1840s that the Magyar nobility – a class consisting of about 136,000 souls monopolizing land and political rights in a country of eleven million people[40] – became seriously committed to Magyarization, and then only to prevent its own historic marginalization.

At the same time, slowly increasing literacy (by 1869 one third of the adult population), the spread of print-Magyar, and the growth of a small, but energetic, liberal intelligentsia all stimulated a *popular* Hungarian nationalism conceived very differently from that of the nobility. This popular nationalism, symbolized for later generations by the figure of Lajos Kossuth (1802–1894), had its hour of glory in the Revolution of 1848. The revolutionary regime not only got rid of the imperial governors appointed by Vienna, but abolished the supposedly Ur-Magyar feudal Diet of Noble Counties, and proclaimed reforms to put an end to serfdom and noblemen's tax-exempt status, as well as to curb drastically the entailment

38. Ignotus, *Hungary*, pp. 47–48. Thus in 1820 the *Tiger im Schlafrock* (Tiger in a Nightgown), Emperor Franz II, made a fine impression with his Latin address to the Hungarian magnates assembled in Pest. In 1825 however, the romantic-radical grand seigneur Count István Széchenyi 'staggered his fellow-magnates' in the Diet by addressing them in Magyar! Jászi, *The Dissolution*, p. 80; and Ignotus, *Hungary*, p. 51.

39. Translated citation from his *The Old Hungary* (1910) in Jászi, *The Dissolution*, pp. 70–71. Grünwald (1839–1891) was an interesting and tragic figure. Born to a Magyarized noble family of Saxon descent, he became both a superb administrator and one of Hungary's earliest social scientists. The publication of his research demonstrating that the famous Magyar gentry-controlled 'counties' were parasites on the nation evoked a savage campaign of public obloquy. He fled to Paris and there drowned himself in the Seine. Ignotus, *Hungary*, pp. 108–109.

40. Jászi, *The Dissolution*, p. 299.

of estates. In addition, it was decided that all Hungarian-speakers should be Hungarian (as only the privileged had been before) and every Hungarian should speak Magyar (as only some Magyars had hitherto been accustomed to do). As Ignotus dryly comments, 'The "nation" was, by the standard of that time (which viewed the rise of the twin stars of Liberalism and Nationalism with boundless optimism), justified in feeling itself extremely generous when it "admitted" the Magyar peasant with no discrimination save for that relating to property;[41] and the non-Magyar Christians on condition they became Magyar; and eventually, with some reluctance and a delay of twenty years, the Jews.'[42] Kossuth's own position, in his fruitless negotiations with leaders of the various non-Magyar minorities, was that these peoples should have exactly the same civil rights as the Magyars, but that since they lacked 'historical personalities' they could not form nations on their own. Today, this position may seem a trifle arrogant. It will appear in a better light if we recall that the brilliant, young, radical-nationalist poet Sándor Petöfi (1823–1849), a leading spirit of 1848, on one occasion referred to the minorities as 'ulcers on the body of the motherland.'[43]

After the suppression of the revolutionary regime by Czarist armies in August 1849, Kossuth went into life-long exile. The stage was now set for a revival of 'official' Magyar nationalism, epitomized by the reactionary regimes of Count Kálmán Tisza (1875–1890) and his son István (1903–1906). The reasons for this revival are very instructive. During the 1850s, the authoritarian-bureaucratic Bach administration in Vienna combined severe political repression with a firm implementation of certain social and economic policies proclaimed by the revolutionaries of 1848 (most notably the abolition of serfdom and noblemen's tax-exempt status) and the promotion of modernized communications and large-scale capitalist enterprise.[44] Largely deprived of its feudal privileges and security, and incapable of competing economically with the great latifundists and energetic German and Jewish entrepreneurs, the old middle and lower Magyar nobility declined into an angry, frightened rural gentry.

Luck, however, was on their side. Humiliatingly defeated by Prussian

41. The Kossuth regime instituted adult male suffrage, but with such high property qualifications that relatively few persons were in a position to vote.

42. Ignotus, *Hungary*, p. 56.

43. Ibid., p. 59.

44. Ignotus observes that Bach did provide the noblemen with some financial compensation for the loss of their privileges, 'probably neither more or less than they would have got under Kossuth' (pp. 64–65).

armies on the field of Königgrätz in 1866, Vienna was forced to accede to the institution of the Dual Monarchy in the Ausgleich (Compromise) of 1867. From then on, the Kingdom of Hungary enjoyed a very considerable autonomy in the running of its internal affairs. The initial beneficiaries of the Ausgleich were a group of liberal-minded high Magyar aristocrats and educated professionals. In 1868, the administration of the cultivated magnate Count Gyula Andrássy enacted a Nationalities Law which gave the non-Magyar minorities 'every right they had ever claimed or could have claimed – short of turning Hungary into a federation.'[45] But Tisza's accession to the premiership in 1875 opened an era in which the reactionary gentry successfully reconstituted their position, relatively free from Viennese interference.

In the economic field, the Tisza regime gave the great agrarian magnates a free hand,[46] but political power was essentially monopolized by the gentry. For

> there remained only one refuge for the dispossessed: the administrative network of national and local government and the army. For these, Hungary needed a tremendous staff; and if she did not she could at least pretend to. Half the country consisted of 'nationalities' to be kept in check. To pay a host of reliable, Magyar, gentlemanly country magistrates to control them, so the argument ran, was a modest price for the national interest. The problem of multi-nationalities was also a godsend; it excused the proliferation of sinecures.

Thus 'the magnates held their entailed estates: the gentry held their entailed jobs.'[47] Such was the social basis for a pitiless policy of enforced Magyarization which after 1875 made the Nationalities Law a dead letter. Legal narrowing of the suffrage, proliferation of rotten boroughs, rigged elections, and organized political thuggery in the rural areas[48] simultaneously consolidated the power of Tisza and his constituency and underscored the 'official' character of their nationalism.

Jászi rightly compares this late-nineteenth-century Magyarization to 'the policy of Russian Tsardom against the Poles, the Finns, and the Ruthe-

45. Ibid., p. 74.

46. As a result, the number of entailed estates trebled between 1867 and 1918. If one includes Church property, fully one third of all land in Hungary was entailed by the end of the Dual Monarchy. German and Jewish capitalists also did well under Tisza.

47. Ibid., pp. 81 and 82.

48. The thuggery was mainly the work of the notorious 'pandoors,' part of the army put at the disposal of the county administrators and deployed as a violent rural police.

nians; the policy of Prussia against the Poles and Danes; and the policy of feudal England against the Irish.'[49] The nexus of reaction and official nationalism is nicely illustrated by these facts: while linguistic Magyarization was a central element of regime policy, by the end of the 1880s only 2% of the officials in the more important branches of central and local governments were Romanian, although Romanians constituted 20% of the population, and 'even these 2% are employed in the lowest grades.'[50] On the other hand, in the Hungarian parliament prior to World War I, there was 'not a single representative of the working classes and of the landless peasantry (the great majority of the country) . . . and there were only 8 Romanians and Slovaks out of a total membership of 413 in a country in which only 54% of the inhabitants spoke Magyar as their mother-tongue.'[51] Small wonder, then, that when Vienna sent in troops to dissolve this parliament in 1906, 'not even a single mass-meeting, a single placard, or a single popular proclamation protested against the new era of "Viennese absolutism." On the contrary the working masses and nationalities regarded with malicious joy the impotent struggle of the national oligarchy.'[52]

The triumph of the reactionary Magyar gentry's 'official nationalism' after 1875 cannot, however, be explained solely by that group's own political strength, nor by the freedom of manoeuvre it inherited from the Ausgleich. The fact is that until 1906 the Habsburg court did not feel in a position to assert itself decisively against a regime which in many respects remained a pillar of the empire. Above all, the dynasty was incapable of superimposing a strenuous official nationalism of its own. Not merely

49. *The Dissolution*, p. 328.

50. According to the calculations of Lajos Mocsáry (*Some Words on the Nationality Problem*, Budapest, 1886), cited in ibid., pp. 331–332. Mocsáry (1826–1916) had in 1874 established a small Independence Party in the Hungarian parliament to fight for Kossuth's ideas, particularly on the minorities question. His speeches denouncing Tisza's blatant violations of the 1868 Nationalities Law led first to his physical extrusion from parliament and then expulsion from his own party. In 1888, he was returned to parliament from a wholly Romanian constituency and became largely a political outcast. Ignotus, *Hungary*, p. 109.

51. Jászi, *The Dissolution*, p. 334.

52. Ibid., p. 362. Right into the twentieth century there was a spurious quality to this 'national oligarchy.' Jászi reports the diverting story of one correspondent of a famous Hungarian daily who during World War I interviewed the wounded officer who would become the ferociously reactionary dictator of Hungary in the inter-war years. Horthy was enraged by the article's description of his thoughts 'winging back to the Hungarian fatherland, home of the ancestors.' 'Remember,' he said, 'that, if my chief warlord is in Baden, then my fatherland is also there!' *The Dissolution*, p. 142.

because the regime was, in the words of the eminent socialist Viktor Adler, '*Absolutismus gemildert durch Schlamperei* [absolution tempered by slovenliness].'[53] Later than almost anywhere else, the dynasty clung to vanished conceptions. 'In his *religious* mysticism, each Habsburg felt himself connected by a special tie with divinity, as an executor of the divine will. This explains their almost unscrupulous attitude in the midst of historical catastrophes, and their proverbial ungratefulness. *Der Dank vom Hause Habsburg* became a widely spread slogan.'[54] In addition, bitter jealousy of Hohenzollern Prussia, which increasingly made off with the plate of the Holy Roman Empire *and* turned itself into Germany, kept the dynasty insisting on Franz II's splendid 'patriotism for me.'

At the same time, it is interesting that in its last days the dynasty discovered, perhaps to its own surprise, affinities with its Social Democrats, to the point that some of their common enemies spoke sneeringly of 'Burgsozialismus [Court Socialism]'. In this tentative coalition there was doubtless a mixture of Machiavellism and idealism on each side. One can see this mixture in the vehement campaign led by the Austrian Social Democrats against the economic and military 'separatism' pressed by the regime of Count István Tisza in 1905. Karl Renner, for example, 'chastized the cowardice of the Austrian bourgeoisie who began to acquiesce in the separatistic plans of the Magyars, though "the Hungarian market is incomparably more significant *for Austrian capital* than [the] Moroccan is for the German," which German foreign policy defends so energetically. In the claim for an independent Hungarian customs territory, he saw nothing else than the clamouring of city sharks, swindlers, and political demagogues, against the *very interests of Austrian industry*, of the Austrian

53. Ibid., p. 165. 'And in the good old days when there was still such a place as Imperial Austria, one could leave the train of events, get into an ordinary train on an ordinary railway-line, and travel back home . . . . Of course cars also drove along those roads – but not too many cars! The conquest of the air had begun here too; but not too intensively. Now and then a ship was sent off to South America or the Far East; but not too often. There was no ambition to have world markets and world power. Here one was in the centre of Europe, at the focal point of the world's old axes; the words 'colony' and 'overseas' had the ring of something as yet utterly untried and remote. There was some display of luxury, but it was not, of course, as oversophisticated as the French. One went in for sport; but not in madly Anglo-Saxon fashion. One spent tremendous sums on the army; but only just enough to assure one of remaining the second weakest among the great powers.' Robert Musil, *The Man Without Qualities*, I, pp. 31–32. This book is the great comic novel of our century.

54. Jászi, *The Dissolution*, p. 135. Author's emphasis. When Metternich was dismissed after the 1848 insurrections and had to flee, 'nobody in the whole court asked him where he would go and how he could live.' Sic transit.

working-classes, and of the Hungarian agricultural population.'[55] Similarly, Otto Bauer wrote that:[56]

> To curb the country [Hungary], split by class and national antagonisms, by sheer military force, in the period of the Russian revolution [of 1905], nobody will dare. But the inner conflicts of the country will give to the Crown other opportunities which it will be constrained to utilize if it cannot endure the fate of the Bernadotte dynasty: it cannot remain the organ of two distinct wills and still rule both Austria and Hungary. Therefore, it must take care that Hungary and Austria should have one will, and *should constitute one empire* . . . . The Crown will not hesitate to send its army to Hungary *to reconquer it for the empire*, but it will write on its flags: Unadulterated, universal suffrage and secret ballot! Right of coalition for the agricultural proletariat! National autonomy! It will oppose to the idea of the independent Hungarian national state the idea of the United States of Greater Austria [sic], the idea of a confederative state in which each nation will administer independently its national affairs and all the nations will unite in one state for the protection of their common interests. Necessarily and inevitably the idea of a confederation of nationalities will become the instrument of the Crown because the dissolution of dualism menaces it with the destruction of its empire . . . .

It seems reasonable to detect in this United States of Greater Austria (USGA) residues of the USA and the United Kingdom of Great Britain and Northern Ireland (one day to be ruled by a Labour Party), as well as a foreshadowing of a Union of Soviet Socialist Republics whose stretch is strangely reminiscent of Czardom's. The fact is that this USGA seemed, in its imaginer's mind, the necessary heir of a *particular* dynastic dominion (Greater Austria) — with its enfranchised components exactly those produced by centuries of Habsburg 'hucksterings'.

Such 'imperial' imaginings were partly the misfortune of a socialism born in the capital of one of Europe's great dynastic empires.[57] As we have noted earlier, the new imagined communities (including the still-born, but still imagined USGA) conjured up by lexicography and print-capitalism always regarded themselves as somehow ancient. In an age in which 'history' itself was still widely conceived in terms of 'great events' and 'great

55. Ibid., p. 181. Emphases added.

56. *Die Nationalitätenfrage und die Sozialdemokratie*, p. 383, as cited and translated in ibid., pp. 181–182. Emphases added.

57. Surely they also reflect the characteristic mindset of a well-known type of leftwing European intellectual, proud of his command of the civilized languages, his Enlightenment heritage, and his penetrating understanding of everyone else's problems. In this pride, internationalist and aristocratic ingredients are rather evenly mixed.

leaders', pearls strung along a thread of narrative, it was obviously tempting to decipher the community's past in antique dynasties. Hence a USGA, in which the membrane separating empire from nation, crown from proletariat, is almost transparent. Nor was Bauer unusual in all this. A William the Conqueror and a George I, neither of whom could speak English, continue to appear unproblematically as beads in the necklace 'Kings of England'. 'Saint' Stephen (r. 1001–1038) might admonish his successor that:[58]

> The utility of foreigners and guests is so great that they can be given a place of sixth importance among the royal ornaments . . . . For, as the guests come from various regions and provinces, they bring with them various languages and customs, various knowledges and arms. All these adorn the royal court, heighten its splendour, and terrify the haughtiness of foreign powers. For a country unified in language and customs is fragile and weak . . . .

But such words would not in the least prevent his subsequent apotheosis as the First King of Hungary.

In conclusion, then, it has been argued that from about the middle of the nineteenth century there developed what Seton-Watson terms 'official nationalisms' inside Europe. These nationalisms were historically 'impossible' until after the appearance of popular linguistic-nationalisms, for, at bottom, they were *responses* by power-groups – primarily, but not exclusively, dynastic and aristocratic – threatened with exclusion from, or marginalization in, popular imagined communities. A sort of tectonic upheaval was beginning, which, after 1918 and 1945, tipped these groups towards drainages in Estoril and Monte Carlo. Such official nationalisms were conservative, not to say reactionary, *policies*, adapted from the model of the largely spontaneous popular nationalisms that preceded them.[59] Nor were they ultimately confined to Europe and the Levant. In the name of imperialism, very similar policies were pursued by the same sorts of groups in the vast Asian and African territories subjected in the course of the nineteenth century.[60] Finally, refracted into non-European cultures and

58. Jászi, *The Dissolution*, p. 39.
59. Half a century ago Jászi had already suspected as much: 'One may ask whether the late imperialist developments of nationalism do really emanate from the genuine sources of the national idea and not from the monopolistic interests of certain groups which were *alien* to the original conception of national aims.' Ibid., p. 286. Emphasis added.
60. The point is nicely underlined by inversion in the case of the Netherlands Indies, which in its last days was still to a large extent ruled through a language which we know today

histories, they were picked up and imitated by indigenous ruling groups in those few zones (among them Japan and Siam) which escaped direct subjection.

In almost every case, official nationalism concealed a discrepancy between nation and dynastic realm. Hence a world-wide contradiction: Slovaks were to be Magyarized, Indians Anglicized, and Koreans Japanified, but they would not be permitted to join pilgrimages which would permit them to administer Magyars, Englishmen, or Japanese. The banquet to which they were invited always turned out to be a Barmecide feast. The reason for all this was not simply racism; it was also the fact that at the core of the empires nations too were emerging – Hungarian, English, and Japanese. And these nations were also instinctively resistant to 'foreign' rule. Imperialist ideology in the post-1850 era thus typically had the character of a conjuring-trick. How much it was a conjuring-trick is suggested by the equanimity with which metropolitan popular classes eventually shrugged off the 'losses' of the colonies, even in cases like Algeria where the colony had been legally incorporated into the metropole. In the end, it is always the ruling classes, bourgeois certainly, but above all aristocratic, that long mourn the empires, and their grief always has a stagey quality to it.

---

as 'Indonesian.' This is, I think, the only case of a large colonial possession in which to the end a non-European language remained a language-of-state. The anomaly is primarily to be explained by the sheer antiquity of the colony, which was founded early in the seventeenth century by a corporation (the Vereenigde Oostindische Compagnie) – long before the age of official nationalism. Doubtless also there was a certain lack of confidence on the part of the Dutch in modern times that their language and culture had a European cachet comparable to that of English, French, German, Spanish, or Italian. (Belgians in the Congo would use French rather than Vlaamsch.) Finally, colonial educational policy was exceptionally conservative: in 1940, when the indigenous population numbered well over 70 millions, there were only 637 'natives' in college, and only 37 graduated with BAs. See George McT. Kahin, *Nationalism and Revolution in Indonesia*, p. 32. For more on the Indonesian case, see below, Chapter VII.

7
The Last Wave

The First World War brought the age of high dynasticism to an end. By 1922, Habsburgs, Hohenzollerns, Romanovs and Ottomans were gone. In place of the Congress of Berlin came the League of *Nations,* from which non-Europeans were not excluded. From this time on, the legitimate international norm was the nation-state, so that in the League even the surviving imperial powers came dressed in national costume rather than imperial uniform. After the cataclysm of World War II the nation-state tide reached full flood. By the mid-1970s even the Portuguese Empire had become a thing of the past.

The new states of the post-World War II period have their own character, which nonetheless is incomprehensible except in terms of the succession of models we have been considering. One way of underlining this ancestry is to remind ourselves that a very large number of these (mainly non-European) nations came to have European languages-of-state. If they resembled the 'American' model in this respect, they took from linguistic European nationalism its ardent populism, and from official nationalism its Russifying policy-orientation. They did so because Americans and Europeans had lived through complex historical experiences which were now everywhere modularly imagined, and because the European languages-of-state they employed were the legacy of imperialist official nationalism. This is why so often in the 'nation-building' policies of the new states one sees both a genuine, popular nationalist enthusiasm and a systematic, even Machiavellian, instilling of nationalist ideology through the mass media, the educational system, administrative regulations, and so forth. In turn, this blend of popular and official nationalism has been the product of anomalies created by European imperialism: the well-known arbitrariness of frontiers, and bilingual intelligentsias poised precariously over diverse monoglot populations. One can thus think of many of these nations as projects the achievement of which is still in progress, yet projects conceived more in the spirit of Mazzini than that of Uvarov.

In considering the origins of recent 'colonial nationalism', one central similarity with the colonial nationalisms of an earlier age immediately strikes the eye: the isomorphism between each nationalism's territorial stretch and that of the previous imperial administrative unit. The similarity is by no means fortuitous; it is clearly related to the geography of all colonial pilgrimages. The difference lies in the fact that the contours of eighteenth-century creole pilgrimages were shaped not only by the centralizing ambitions of metropolitan absolutism, but by real problems of communication and transportation, and a general technological primitiveness. In the twentieth century, these problems had largely been overcome, and in their place came a Janus-faced 'Russification'.

I argued earlier that in the late eighteenth century the imperial administrative unit came to acquire a national meaning in part because it circumscribed the ascent of creole functionaries. So too in the twentieth century. For even in cases where a young brown or black Englishman came to receive some education or training in the metropole, in a way that few of his creole progenitors had been able to do, that was typically the last time he made this bureaucratic pilgrimage. From then on, the apex of his looping flight was *the highest administrative centre to which he could be assigned:* Rangoon, Accra, Georgetown, or Colombo. Yet in each constricted journey he found bilingual travelling companions with whom he came to feel a growing communality. In his journey he understood rather quickly that his point of origin – conceived either ethnically, linguistically, or geographically – was of small significance. At most it started him on this pilgrimage rather than that: it did not fundamentally determine his destination or his companions. Out of this pattern came that subtle, half-concealed transformation, step by step, of the colonial-state into the national-state, a transformation made possible not only by a solid continuity of personnel, but by the established skein of journeys through which each state was experienced by its functionaries.[1]

1. Not only, of course by functionaries, though they were the main group. Consider, for example, the geography of *Noli Me Tangere* (and many other nationalist novels). Though some of the most important characters in Rizal's text are Spanish, and some of the Filipino characters have been to Spain (off the novel's stage), the circumambience of travel by any of the characters is confined to what, eleven years after its publication and two years after its author's execution, would become the Republic of the Philippines.

Yet increasingly after the middle of the nineteenth century, and above all in the twentieth, the journeys were no longer made by only a handful of travellers, but by huge and variegated crowds. The central factors at work were three. First and foremost was the enormous increase in physical mobility made possible by the astonishing achievements of industrial capitalism – railways and steamships in the last century, motor transport and aviation in this. The interminable journeys of the old Americas were quickly becoming things of the past.

Second, imperial 'Russification' has its practical as well as ideological side. The sheer size of the global European empires, and the vast populations subjected, meant that purely metropolitan, or even creole, bureaucracies were neither recruitable nor affordable. The colonial state, and, somewhat later, corporate capital, needed armies of clerks, who to be useful had to be bilingual, capable of mediating linguistically between the metropolitan nation and the colonized peoples. The need was all the greater as the specialized functions of the state everywhere multiplied after the turn of the century. Alongside the old district officer appeared the medical officer, the irrigation engineer, the agricultural extension-worker, the schoolteacher, the policeman, and so on. With every enlargement of the state, the swarm of its inner pilgrims swelled.[2]

Third was the spread of modern-style education, not only by the colonial state, but also by private religious and secular organizations. This expansion occurred not simply to provide cadres for governmental and corporate hierarchies, but also because of the growing acceptance of the moral importance of modern knowledge even for colonized populations.[3] (Indeed the phenomenon of educated unemployed in ex-colonial countries was already beginning to be apparent in a variety of colonial states.)

It is generally recognized that the intelligentsia were central to the rise of nationalism in the colonial territories, not least because colonialism ensured that native agrarian magnates, big merchants, industrial entrepreneurs, and even a large professional class were relative rarities. Almost

2. To give only one example: by 1928, there were almost 250,000 indigenes on the payroll of the Netherlands East Indies, and these formed 90% of all state functionaries. (Symptomatically, the widely discrepant salaries and pensions of Dutch and native officials, when combined, ate up 50% of state expenditures!). See Amry Vandenbosch, *The Dutch East Indies*, pp. 171–73. Yet Dutchmen were proportionately nine times as thick on the bureaucratic ground as were Englishmen in British (non-'native state') India.

3. Even in the ultra-conservative Netherlands Indies, the numbers of natives receiving a primary Western-style education shot up from an average of 2,987 in the years 1900–04 to 74,697 in 1928; while those receiving a Western-style secondary education increased in the same span of time from 25 to 6,468. Kahin, *Nationalism*, p. 31.

everywhere economic power was either monopolized by the colonialists themselves, or unevenly shared with a politically impotent class of pariah (non-native) businessmen – Lebanese, Indian and Arab in colonial Africa, Chinese, Indian, and Arab in colonial Asia. It is no less generally recognized that the intelligentsia's vanguard role derived from its bilingual literacy, or rather literacy and bilingualism. Print-literacy already made possible the imagined community floating in homogeneous, empty time of which we have spoken earlier. Bilingualism meant access, through the European language-of-state, to modern Western culture in the broadest sense, and, in particular, to the models of nationalism, nation-ness, and nation-state produced elsewhere in the course of the nineteenth century.[4]

In 1913, the Dutch colonial regime in Batavia, taking its lead from The Hague, sponsored massive colony-wide festivities to celebrate the centennial of the 'national liberation' of the Netherlands from French imperialism. Orders went out to secure physical participation and financial contributions, not merely from the local Dutch and Eurasian communities, but also from the subject native population. In protest, the early Javanese-Indonesian nationalist Suwardi Surjaningrat (Ki Hadjar Dewantoro) wrote his famous Dutch-language newspaper article 'Als ik eens Nederlander was' (If I were temporarily to be a Dutchman).[5]

> In my opinion, there is something out of place – something indecent – if we (I still being a Dutchman in my imagination) ask the natives to join the festivities which celebrate our independence. Firstly, we will hurt their sensitive feelings because we are here celebrating our own independence in their native country which we colonize. At the moment we are very happy because a hundred years ago we liberated ourselves from foreign domination; and all of this is occurring in front of the eyes of those who are still under our domination. Does it not occur to us that these poor slaves are also longing for such a moment as this, when they like us will be able to celebrate their independence? Or do we perhaps feel that because of our soul-destroying policy we regard all human souls as dead? If that is so, then we are deluding ourselves, because no matter how primitive a community is, it is against any type of

4. To borrow from Anthony Barnett, it also 'allowed the intellectuals to *say* to their fellow-speakers [of the indigenous vernaculars] that "we" can be like "them"'.

5. It appeared originally in *De Expres* on July 13, 1913, but was quickly translated into 'Indonesian' and published in the native press. Suwardi was then 24 years old. An unusually well-educated and progressive aristocrat, he had in 1912 joined with a Javanese commoner, Dr. Tjipto Mangoenkoesoemo, and a Eurasian, Eduard Douwes Dekker, to form the Indische Partij, the colony's first political party. For a brief, but useful, study of Suwardi, see Savitri Scherer, 'Harmony and Dissonance: Early Nationalist Thought in Java', chapter 2. Her Appendix I gives an English translation of the famous article, from which this passage is drawn.

oppression. If I were a Dutchman, I would not organize an independence celebration in a country where the independence of the people has been stolen.

With these words Suwardi was able to turn Dutch history against the Dutch, by scraping boldly at the weld between Dutch nationalism and imperialism. Furthermore, by the imaginary transformation of himself into a temporary Dutchman (which invited a reciprocal transformation of his Dutch readers into temporary Indonesians), he undermined all the racist fatalities that underlay Dutch colonial ideology.[6]

Suwardi's broadside — which delighted his Indonesian as much as it irritated his Dutch audience — is exemplary of a world-wide twentieth-century phenomenon. For the paradox of imperial official nationalism was that it inevitably brought what were increasingly thought of and written about as European 'national histories' into the consciousnesses of the colonized — not merely via occasional obtuse festivities, but also through reading-rooms and classrooms.[7] Vietnamese youngsters could not avoid learning about the *philosophes* and the Revolution, and what Debray calls 'our secular antagonism to Germany'.[8] Magna Carta, the Mother of Parliaments, and the Glorious Revolution, glossed as English national history, entered schools all over the British Empire. Belgium's independence struggle against Holland was not erasable from school-books Congolese children would one day read. So also the histories of the USA in the Philippines and, last of all, Portugal in Mozambique and Angola. The irony, of course, is that these histories were written out of a historiographical consciousness which by the turn of the century was, all over Europe, becoming nationally-defined. (The barons who imposed Magna Carta on John Plantagenet did not speak 'English,' and had no conception of themselves as 'Englishmen,' but they were firmly defined as early patriots in the classrooms of the United Kingdom 700 years later.)

Yet there is a characteristic feature of the emerging nationalist intelligentsias in the colonies which to some degree marks them off from the

6. Notice the educational linkage here between 'imagined' and 'imaginary' communities.

7. The celebrations of 1913 were agreeably emblematic of official nationalism in another sense. The 'national liberation' commemorated was in fact the restoration of the House of Orange by the victorious armies of the Holy Alliance (not the establishment of the Batavian Republic in 1795); and half the liberated nation soon seceded to form the Kingdom of Belgium in 1830. But the 'national liberation' gloss was certainly what Suwardi imbibed in his colonial classroom.

8. 'Marxism and the National Question,' p. 41.

vernacularizing nationalist intelligentsias of nineteenth-century Europe. Almost invariably they were very young, and attached a complex political significance to their youth – a significance which, though it has changed over time, remains important to this day. The rise of (modern/organized) Burmese nationalism is often dated to the founding in 1908 of the Young Men's Buddhist Association in Rangoon; and of Malayan by the establishment in 1938 of the Kesatuan Melayu Muda (Union of Malay Youth). Indonesians annually celebrate the *Sumpah Pemuda* (Oath of Youth) drawn up and sworn by the nationalist youth congress of 1928. And so on. It is perfectly true that in one sense Europe had been there before – if we think of Young Ireland, Young Italy, and the like. Both in Europe and in the colonies 'young' and 'youth' signified dynamism, progress, self-sacrificing idealism and revolutionary will. But, on the whole, in Europe 'young' had little in the way of definable sociological contours. Once could be middle-aged and still part of Young Ireland; one could be illiterate and still part of Young Italy. The reason, of course, was that the language of these nationalisms was either a vernacular mother-tongue to which the members had spoken access from the cradle, or, as in the case of Ireland, a metropolitan language which had sunk such deep roots in sections of the population over centuries of conquest that it too could manifest itself, creole-style, as a vernacular. There was thus no necessary connection between language, age, class, or status.

In the colonies things were very different. Youth meant, above all, the *first* generation in any significant numbers to have acquired a European education, marking them off linguistically and culturally from their parents' generation, as well from the vast bulk of their colonized agemates (cf. B. C. Pal). Burma's 'English-language' YMBA, modelled in part on the YMCA, was built by English-reading schoolboys. In the Netherlands Indies one finds, *inter alia,* Jong Java (Young Java), Jong Ambon (Young Amboina), and Jong Islamietenbond (League of Young Muslims) – titles incomprehensible to any young native unacquainted with the colonial tongue.

In the colonies, then, by 'Youth' we mean 'Schooled Youth,' at least at the start. This in turns reminds us again of the unique role played by colonial school-systems in promoting colonial nationalisms.[9]

9. Our focus here will be on civilian schools. But their military counterparts were often important too. The professionally officered standing army pioneered by Prussia early in the nineteenth century has required an educational pyramid in some ways more elaborate, if not

The case of Indonesia affords a fascinatingly intricate illustration of this process, not least because of its enormous size, huge population (even in colonial times), geographical fragmentation (about 3,000 islands), religious variegation (Muslims, Buddhists, Catholics, assorted Protestants, Hindu-Balinese, and 'animists'), and ethnolinguistic diversity (well over 100 distinct groups). Furthermore, as its hybrid pseudo-Hellenic name suggests, its stretch does not remotely correspond to any precolonial domain; on the contrary, at least until General Suharto's brutal invasion of ex-Portuguese East Timor in 1975, its boundaries have been those left behind by the last Dutch conquests (c. 1910).

Some of the peoples on the eastern coast of Sumatra are not only physically close, across the narrow Straits of Malacca, to the populations of the western littoral of the Malay Peninsula, but they are ethnically related, understand each other's speech, have a common religion, and so forth. These same Sumatrans share neither mother-tongue, ethnicity, nor religion with the Ambonese, located on islands thousands of miles away to the east. Yet during this century they have come to understand the Ambonese as fellow-Indonesians, the Malays as foreigners.

Nothing nurtured this bonding more than the schools that the regime in Batavia set up in increasing numbers after the turn of the century. To see why, one has to remember that in complete contrast to traditional, indigenous schools, which were always local and personal enterprises (even if, in good Muslim fashion, there was plenty of horizontal movement of

---

more specialized, than its civilian analogue. Young officers ('Turks') produced by new military academies have often played significant roles in the development of nationalism. Emblematic is the case of Major Chukuma Nzeogwu, who masterminded the January 15, 1966 coup in Nigeria. A Christian Ibo, he was among the first group of young Nigerians sent for training at Sandhurst to make possible the transformation of a white-officered colonial mercenary force into a national army, on Nigeria's attainment of independence in 1960. (If he attended Sandhurst with the future Brigadier Afrifa, who, also in 1966, was to overthrow *his* government, each native was destined to return to his own imperial habitat). It is striking evidence of the power of the Prussian model that he was able to lead Muslim Hausa troops in assassinating the Sardauna of Sokoto and other Muslim Hausa aristocrats, and, consequently, destroy the Muslim-Hausa-dominated government of Abubakar Tafawa Balewa, It is no less striking a sign of colonial-school-generated nationalism that over Radio Kaduna he assured his countrymen that 'you will no more be ashamed to say that you are Nigerian.' (Quotation taken from Anthony H. M. Kirk-Greene, *Crisis and Conflict in Nigeria: A Documentary Source Book*, p. 126.) Yet nationalism was thinly enough then spread in Nigeria for Nzeogwu's nationalist coup to be quickly interpreted as an Ibo plot; hence the military mutinies of July, the anti-Ibo pogroms of September and October, and Biafra's secession in May 1967. (See Robin Luckham's superb *The Nigerian Military*, passim.)

students from one particularly well-reputed ulama-teacher to another), the government schools formed a colossal, highly rationalized, tightly-centralized hierarchy, structurally analogous to the state bureaucracy itself. Uniform textbooks, standardized diplomas and teaching certificates, a tightly regulated gradation of age-groups,[10] classes and instructional materials, in themselves created a self-contained, coherent universe of experience. But no less important was the hierarchy's geography. Standardized elementary schools came to be scattered about in villages and small townships of the colony; junior and senior middle-schools in larger towns and provincial centres; while tertiary education (the pyramid's apex) was confined to the colonial capital of Batavia and the Dutch-built city of Bandung, 100 miles southwest in the cool Priangan highlands. Thus the twentieth-century colonial school-system brought into being pilgrimages which paralleled longer-established functionary journeys. The Rome of these pilgrimages was Batavia: not Singapore, not Manila, not Rangoon, not even the old Javanese royal capitals of Jogjakarta and Surakarta.[11] From all over the vast colony, but from nowhere outside it, the tender pilgrims made their inward, upward way, meeting fellow-pilgrims from different, perhaps once hostile, villages in primary school; from different ethnolinguistic groups in middle-school; and from every part of the realm in the tertiary institutions of the capital.[12] And they knew that from wherever they had come they still had read the same books and done the same sums. They also knew, even if they never got so far – and most did not – that Rome was Batavia, and that all these journeyings derived their 'sense' from the capital, in effect explaining why 'we' are 'here' 'together.' To put it another way, their common experience, and the amiably competitive comradeship of the classroom, gave the maps of the colony which they studied (always coloured differently from British Malaya or the American Philippines) a territorially-specific imagined reality which was every day confirmed by the accents and physiognomies of their classmates.[13]

10. The idea of a student being 'too old' to be in class X or Y, unthinkable in a traditional Muslim school, was an unselfconscious axiom of the colonial Western-style school.

11. Ultimately, of course, the apices were The Hague, Amsterdam, and Leiden; but those who could seriously dream of studying there were a tiny handful.

12. Being secular, twentieth-century schools they were usually co-educational, though with boys the preponderant majority. Hence love-affairs, and quite often marriages, 'off the school-bench,' which crossed all traditional lines.

13. Sukarno never saw the West Irian for which he fought so hard till he was over 60. Here, as in the schoolroom maps, we see fiction seeping into reality – cf. *Noli* and *El Periquillo Sarniento*.

And what were they all together? The Dutch were quite clear on this point: whatever mother-tongue they spoke, they were irremediably *inlanders,* a word which, like the English 'natives' and the French *'indigènes,'* always carried an unintentionally paradoxical semantic load. In this colony, as in each separate, other colony, it meant that the persons referred to were both 'inferior' *and 'belonged there'* (just as the Dutch, being 'natives' of Holland, belonged *there*). Conversely, the Dutch by such language assigned themselves, along with superiority, 'not-belonging-there'. The word also implied that in their common inferiority, the *inlanders* were *equally* contemptible, no matter what ethnolinguistic group or class they came from. Yet even this miserable equality of condition had a definite perimeter. For *inlander* always raised the question 'native of what?' If the Dutch sometimes spoke as if *inlanders* were a world-category, experience showed that this notion was hardly sustainable in practice. *Inlanders* stopped at the coloured colony's drawn edge. Beyond that were, variously, 'natives,' *indigènes* and *indios.* Moreover, colonial legal terminology included the category *vreemde oosterlingen* (foreign Orientals), which had the dubious ring of false coin – as it were 'foreign natives.' Such 'foreign Orientals,' mainly Chinese, Arabs and Japanese, though they might live in the colony, had a politico-legal status superior to that of the 'native natives'. Furthermore, tiny Holland was sufficiently awed by the Meiji oligarchs' economic strength and military prowess for Japanese in the colony to be legally promoted, from 1899 on, to 'honorary Europeans'. From all this, by a sort of sedimentation, *inlander* – excluding whites, Dutchmen, Chinese, Arabs, Japanese, 'natives,' *indigènes*, and *Indios* – grew ever more specific in content; until, like a ripe larva, it was suddenly transmogrified into the spectacular butterfly called 'Indonesian'.

While it is true that the concepts *inlander* and 'native' could never be truly generalized racist notions, since they always implied roots in some specific habitat,[14] the case of Indonesia should not lead us to assume that each 'native' habitat had preordained or immutable frontiers. Two examples will show the contrary: French West Africa and French Indochina.

In its heyday, the École Normale William Ponty in Dakar, though only a secondary school, was still the apex of the colonial educational pyramid in

---

14. Compare, by contrast, 'half-breeds' or 'niggers,' who, beginning at Calais, can crop up anywhere on the planet outside the United Kingdom.

French West Africa.[15] To William Ponty came intelligent students from what we know today as Guinea, Mali, the Ivory Coast, Senegal, and so on. We should not be surprised therefore if the pilgrimages of these boys, terminating in Dakar, were initially read in French [West] African terms, of which the paradoxical concept *négritude* – essence of African-ness express-ible only in French, language of the William Ponty classrooms – is an unforgettable symbol. Yet the apicality of William Ponty was accidental and evanescent. As more secondary schools were constructed in French West Africa, it was no longer necessary for bright boys to make so distant a pilgrimage. And in any case the educational centrality of William Ponty was never matched by a comparable administrative centrality of Dakar. The interchangeability of French West African boys on the benches of William Ponty was not paralleled by their later bureaucratic substitutability in the French West African colonial administration. Hence, the school's Old Boys went home to become, eventually, Guinean or Malian nationalist leaders, while retaining a 'West African' camaraderie and solidary intimacy lost to succeeding generations.[16]

In much the same way, for one generation of relatively well-educated adolescents, the curious hybrid 'Indochine' had a real, experienced,

15. On the origins and development of this famous school, see Abdou Moumouni, *L'Edu-cation en Afrique*, pp. 41–49; on its political significance, Ruth Schachter Morgenthau, *Political Parties in French-Speaking West Africa*, pp. 12–14, 18–21. Originally an untitled *école normale* located in Saint-Louis, it was moved to Gorée, just outside Dakar, in 1913. Subse-quently it was named after William Merlaud-Ponty, the fourth governor-general (1908–15) of French West Africa. Serge Thion informs me that the name William (as opposed to Guillaume) has long been in vogue in the area around Bordeaux. He is surely right in attributing this popularity to the historic ties with England created by the wine trade; but it seems just possible that it goes back to the era when Bordeaux (Guyenne) was still a solid part of the realm ruled from London.

16. There seems to have been nothing similar in British West Africa, whether because the British colonies were non-contiguous, or because London was wealthy and liberal enough to start secondary schools almost simultaneously in the major territories, or because of the localism of rival Protestant missionary organizations. Achimota School, a secondary school founded by the colonial state in Accra in 1927, quickly became the main peak of a Gold Coast-specific educational pyramid, and after independence it was where the children of cabinet ministers began learning how to succeed their fathers. A rival peak, Mfantsipim Secondary School, had the advantage of seniority (it was founded in 1876), but the weaknesses of locale (Cape Coast) and semi-detachment from the state (it was in denominational hands till well after independence). I owe this information to Mohamed Chambas.

imagined meaning.[17] This entity, it will be recalled, was not legally pro-claimed until 1887, and did not acquire its fullest territorial form until 1907, though active French meddling in the general area went back a century earlier.

Broadly speaking, the educational policy pursued by the colonial rulers of 'Indochine' had two fundamental purposes[18] – both of which, as it turned out, contributed to the growth of an 'Indochinese' consciousness. One aim was to break existing politico-cultural ties between the colonized peoples and the immediate extra-Indochinese world. As far as 'Cambodge' and 'Laos' were concerned,[19] the target was Siam, which had previously exer-cised a variable suzerainty over them and shared with both the rituals, institutions, and sacred language of Hinayana Buddhism. (In addition, the language and script of the lowland Lao were, and are, closely related to those of the Thai.) It was precisely out of this concern that the French experimented first in those zones *last* seized from Siam with the so-called 'renovated pagoda schools,' which were designed to remove Khmer monks and their pupils out of the Thai orbit into that of Indochina.[20]

In eastern Indochina (my shorthand for 'Tonkin,' 'Annam,' and 'Cochin China'), the target was China and Chinese civilization. Although the dynasties ruling in Hanoi and Hué had for centuries defended their inde-pendence from Peking, they came to rule through a mandarinate con-

17. It led, *inter alia,* to a one-generation (1930–1951?) Indochinese Communist Party in which, for a time, youngsters whose mother tongues might be Vietnamese, Khmer, or Lao participated. Today, the formation of this party is sometimes viewed merely as an expression of 'age-old Vietnamese expansionism.' In fact, it was sired by the Comintern out of the educational (and to a lesser extent administrative) system of French Indochina.

18. This policy is ably and thoroughly discussed in Gail Paradise Kelly, 'Franco-Vietnamese Schools, 1918 to 1938'. Unluckily, the author concentrates exclusively on the Vietnamese-speaking population of Indochina.

19. I use this perhaps clumsy terminology to emphasize the colonial origins of these entities. 'Laos' was assembled out of a cluster of rival principalities, leaving more than half of the Lao-speaking population in Siam. The boundaries of 'Cambodge' conformed neither to any particular historical stretch of the precolonial realm, nor to the distribution of the Khmer-speaking peoples. Some hundreds of thousands of such people ended up trapped in 'Cochin China,' producing in time that distinct community known as the Khmer Krom (down-river Khmer).

20. They pursued this aim by establishing in the 1930s an Ecole Supérieure de Pali in Phnom Penh, an ecclesiastical college attended by both Khmer- and Lao-speaking monks. The attempt to turn Buddhist eyes away from Bangkok seems not to have been wholly successful. In 1942 (shortly after Siam regained control of much of northwestern 'Cambodge' with Japanese assistance), the French arrested a venerable professor of the Ecole for possession and distribution of 'subversive' Thai educational materials. (Most likely, these materials were some of the strongly nationalist school-texts produced by the vociferously anti-French regime of Field-Marshal Plaek Phibunsongkhram (1938–1944.)

sciously modelled on that of the Chinese. This meant that recruitment into the state machinery was geared to written examinations in the Confucian classics; dynastic documents were written in Chinese characters; and the ruling class was heavily Sinicized in culture. These long-standing ties assumed an additionally unwelcome character after about 1895, when the writings of such Chinese reformers as K'ang Yu-wei and Liang Ch'i-ch'ao, and nationalists like Sun Yat-sen, began seeping across the northern frontier of the colony.[21] Accordingly, Confucian examinations were successively abolished in 'Tonkin' in 1915 and in 'Annam' in 1918. Henceforth, recruitment into the civil services of Indochina was to take place exclusively through a developing French colonial education system. Furthermore, *quốc ngũ*, a romanized phonetic script originally devised by Jesuit missionaries in the seventeenth century,[22] and adopted by the authorities for use in 'Cochin China' as early as the 1860s, was consciously promoted to break the links with China – and perhaps also with the indigenous past by making dynastic records and ancient literatures inaccessible to a new generation of colonized Vietnamese.[23]

The second aim of educational policy was to produce a carefully-calibrated quantum of French-speaking and French-writing Indochinese to serve as a politically reliable, grateful, and acculturated indigenous elite, filling the subordinate echelons of the colony's bureaucracy and larger commercial enterprises.[24]

---

21. David G. Marr, *Vietnamese Tradition on Trial, 1920–1945*, p. 146. No less alarming were smuggled Chinese translations of such troubling French authors as Rousseau. (Kelly, *Franco-Vietnamese Schools*, p. 19.)

22. In its final form, this script is usually attributed to the gifted lexicographer Alexandre de Rhodes, who in 1651 published his remarkable *Dictionarium annamiticum, lusitanum et latinum*.

23. '[Most] French colonial officials of the late nineteenth century . . . were convinced that to achieve permanent colonial success required the harsh curtailment of Chinese influences, including the writing system. Missionaries often saw the Confucian literati as the main obstacle to the general Catholic conversion of Vietnam. Hence, in their view, to eliminate the Chinese language was simultaneously to isolate Vietnam from its heritage and to neutralize the traditional elite.' (Marr, *Vietnamese Tradition*, p. 145.) Kelly quotes one colonial writer thus: 'in effect, the teaching of quoc ngu alone . . . will have the result of communicating to Vietnamese only the French writing, literature, and philosophy which we wish them [to be exposed to]. That is those [works] which we judge useful to them and easily assimilable: only the texts which we transcribe into quoc ngu.' *Franco-Vietnamese Schools*, p. 22.

24. See Ibid., pp. 14–15. For a wider, lower stratum of the Indochinese population Governor-General Albert Sarraut (author of the 1917 Code of Public Instruction) urged: 'a simple education, reduced to essentials, permitting the child to learn all that will be useful to him to know in his humble career of farmer or artisan to ameliorate the natural and social conditions of his existence.' Ibid., p. 17.

The intricacies of the colonial educational system need not detain us here. For our present purposes, the key characteristic of the system was that it formed a single, if ramshackle, pyramid, of which, until the mid-1930s, the upper terraces all lay in the east. Up until then, for example, the only state-sponsored *lycées* were located in Hanoi and Saigon; and throughout the prewar colonial period, the sole university in Indochina was located in Hanoi, so to speak 'just down the street' from the palace of the Governor-General.[25] The climbers of these terraces included all the major vernacular-speakers of the French domain: Vietnamese, Chinese, Khmer, and Lao (and not a few young French colonials). For the climbers, coming from, shall we say, My Tho, Battambang, Vientiane, and Vinh, the meaning of their convergence had to be 'Indochinese,' in the same way that the polyglot and polyethnic student body of Batavia and Bandung had to read theirs as 'Indonesian.'[26] This Indochinese-ness, although it was quite real, was nonetheless imagined by a tiny group, and not for very long. Why did it turn out to be so evanescent, while Indonesian-ness survived and deepened?

First there was a marked change of course in colonial education, above all as applied in eastern Indochina, from about 1917 on. The actual, or immediately impending. liquidation of the traditional Confucian examination system persuaded more and more members of the Vietnamese elite to try to place their children in the best French schools available, so as to ensure their bureaucratic futures. The resulting competition for places in the few good schools available aroused a particularly strong reaction from the *colons,* who regarded these schools as by right a largely French preserve.

25. In 1937, a total of 631 students were enrolled, 580 of them in the faculties of law and medicine. Ibid., p. 79; see also pp. 69–79, for the bizarre history of this institution, founded in 1906, closed in 1908, reopened in 1918, and never, till the late 1930s, much more than a glorified vocational college.

26. As I shall be concentrating on Khmers and Vietnamese below, this may be the place to make a brief reference to some prominent Lao. The present Prime Minister of Laos, Kaysone Phoumvihan attended the University of Hanoi's medical faculty in the late 1930s. The head of state, Prince Souphanouvong, graduated from Hanoi's Lycée Albert Sarraut before obtaining an engineering degree in metropolitan France. His elder brother, Prince Phetsarath Ratanavongsa, who headed the short-lived Lao Issara (Free Lao) anticolonial government in Vientiane from October 1945 to April 1946, had as a youth been graduated from Saigon's Lycée Chasseloup-Laubat. Prior to World War II, the highest educational institution in 'Laos' was the small Collège [i.e. junior high school] Pavie in Vientiane. See Joseph J. Zasloff, *Pathet Lao*, pp. 104–105; and '3349' [pseudonym of Phetsarath Ratanavongsa], *Iron Man of Laos*, pp. 12 and 46. It is revealing, I think, that in his account of his later schooldays in Paris, Phetsarath regularly and unselfconsciously speaks of his identifiably Lao, Khmer, and Vietnamese classmates as 'the Indochinese students.' See, e.g., ibid., pp. 14–15.

The colonial regime's solution to the problem was to create a separate and subordinate 'Franco-Vietnamese' educational structure which placed special emphasis, in its lower grades, on Vietnamese-language instruction in *quốc ngũ* (with French taught as a second language via the medium of *quốc ngũ*).[27] This policy shift had two complementary results. On the one hand, government publication of hundreds of thousands of *quốc ngũ* primers significantly accelerated the spread of this European-invented script, unintentionally helping to turn it, between 1920 and 1945, into *the* popular medium for the expression of Vietnamese cultural (and national) solidarity.[28] For even if only 10% of the Vietnamese-speaking population was literate by the late 1930s, this was a proportion unprecedented in the history of this people. Moreover, these literates were, unlike the Confucian literati, deeply committed to a rapid increase in their own numbers. (Similarly, in 'Cambodge' and 'Laos,' if on a more limited scale, the authorities promoted the *printing* of elementary school-texts in the vernaculars, initially and mainly in the traditional orthographies, later and more feebly in romanized scripts).[29] On the other hand, the policy worked to exclude non-native-Vietnamese-speakers residing in eastern Indochina. In the case of the Khmer Krom of 'Cochin China,' it worked, in combination with the colonial regime's willingness to permit them to have 'Franco-Khmer' elementary schools like those being encouraged in the Protectorate, to re-orient ambitions *back* up the Mekong. Thus those Khmer Krom adolescents who aspired to higher education in the administrative capital of Indochina (and, for a select few, even in metropolitan France) increasingly took the detour via Phnom Penh rather than the highway through Saigon.

27. Thus in the previously 'integrated' *lycées* Chasseloup-Laubat and Albert Sarraut, substandard 'native sections' were established in 1917–1918. These 'native sections' eventually turned respectively into the Lycée Petrus Ky and the Lycée du Protectorat. (Ibid., pp. 60–63). Nonetheless, a minority of privileged *indigènes* continued to attend the 'real French' *lycées* (the adolescent Norodom Sihanouk graced Chasseloup-Laubat), while a minority of 'French' (mainly Eurasians and natives with French legal status) attended Petrus Ky and its sister institution in Hanoi.

28. Marr notes that in the 1920s 'even the most optimistic member of the intelligentsia [committed to *quốc ngũ*] could not have guessed that only two decades later, citizens of a Democratic Republic of Vietnam would be able to conduct all important affairs – political, military, economic, scientific and academic – in spoken Vietnamese linked to the *quốc ngũ* writing system.' *Vietnamese Tradition*, p. 150. It was also a disagreeable surprise to the French.

29. It is instructive that one of the first issues raised by the early Khmer nationalists of the late 1930s was the 'menace' of a so-called 'quoc ngu-ization' of the Khmer script by the colonial authorities.

Second, in 1935 the Collège Sisowath in Phnom Penh was upgraded into a full-fledged state *lycée,* with a status equal to, *and a curriculum identical with*, those of the existing state *lycées* in Saigon and Hanoi. Although its students were at first drawn heavily (in the tradition of the Collège) from local Sino-Khmer merchant families and those of resident Vietnamese functionaries, the proportion of native Khmers steadily increased.[30] It is probably fair to say that, after 1940, the great bulk of Khmer-speaking adolescents who achieved a solid French high-school education did so in the neat colonial capital the colonialists had built for the Norodoms.

Third was the fact that there was no real isomorphism between the educational and administrative pilgrimages in Indochina. The French made no bones about expressing the view that if the Vietnamese were untrustworthy and grasping, they were nonetheless decisively more energetic and intelligent than the 'child-like' Khmer and Lao. Accordingly, they made extensive use of Vietnamese functionaries in western Indochina.[31] The 176,000 Vietnamese residing in 'Cambodge' in 1937 – representing less than 1% of the 19 million Vietnamese-speakers of the colony, but about 6% of the Protectorate's population – formed a relatively successful group, for whom therefore Indochina had a rather solid meaning, as it did for the 50,000 sent into 'Laos' prior to 1945. Particularly the functionaries among them, who might be posted from place to place in *all five* subsections of the colony, could well imagine Indochina as the wide stage on which they would continue to perform.

Such imagining was much less easy for Lao and Khmer functionaries, although there was no formal or legal prohibition on fully-Indochinese careers for them. Even the more ambitious youngsters coming from the c. 326,000 (1937) Khmer Krom community in eastern Indochina (representing perhaps 10% of the entire Khmer-speaking population) found that *in practice* they had very limited career prospects outside 'Cambodge'. Thus Khmer and Lao might sit alongside Vietnamese in French-language secondary and tertiary schools in Saigon and Hanoi, but they were unlikely to go

30. The pattern was not immediately followed in Vientiane. Toye reports that in the course of the 1930s only 52 Lao were graduated from the Collège [he wrongly terms it Lycée] Pavie, as opposed to 96 Vietnamese. *Laos,* p.45.

31. It is possible that this influx paralleled the institution of the Franco-Vietnamese school system, in that it deflected Vietnamese from competing with French nationals in the more advanced, eastern parts of Indochina. In 1937, there were 39,000 Europeans living in 'Cochin China,' 'Annam' and 'Tonkin,' and only 3,100 in 'Cambodge' and 'Laos' combined. Marr, *Vietnamese Tradition,* p. 23.

on to share administrative offices there. Like youngsters from Cotonou and Abidjan in Dakar, they were destined to go back, on graduation, to the 'homes' colonialism had demarcated for them. To put it another way, if their educational pilgrimages were directed towards Hanoi, their administrative journeys ended in Phnom Penh and Vientiane.

Out of these contradictions emerged those Khmer-speaking students who subsequently came to be remembered as the first Cambodian nationalists. The man who can reasonably be regarded as the 'father' of Khmer nationalism, Son Ngoc Thanh, was, as his Vietnamized name suggests, a Khmer Krom who was educated in Saigon and for a while held a minor judicial post in that city. But in the mid-1930s he abandoned the Paris of the Mekong Delta to seek a more promising future in its Blois. Prince Sisowath Youtevong attended secondary school in Saigon before leaving for France for further study. When he returned to Phnom Penh fifteen years later, after World War II, he helped to found the (Khmer) Democratic Party and served as Prime Minister in 1946–1947. His Defence Minister, Sonn Voeunnsai, undertook virtually the same journeys. Huy Kanthoul, Democratic Prime Minister in 1951–1952, had graduated from an *école normale* in Hanoi in 1931, and was then returned to Phnom Penh, where he eventually joined the Lycée Sisowath's teaching staff.[32] Perhaps most exemplary of all is the figure of Ieu Koeus, first of a melancholy line of assassinated Khmer political leaders.[33] Born in the province of Battambang in 1905 – when it was still ruled from Bangkok – he attended a local 'reformed pagoda school' before entering an 'Indochinese' elementary school in Battambang town. In 1921, he proceeded to the Collège Sisowath in the Protectorate's capital, and then to a *collège de commerce* in Hanoi, from which he graduated in 1927 at the top of his French-reading class. Hoping to study chemistry in Bordeaux, he took and passed the scholarship examination. But the colonial state blocked his way abroad. He returned to his native Battambang, where he ran a pharmacy, continuing to do so even after Bangkok regained the province in 1941. After the Japanese collapse in August 1945, he reappeared in 'Cambodge' as a Democratic parliamentarian. It is notable that he was in his way a lineal descendent of the illustrious philologists of an earlier Europe, insofar as he designed a typwriter keyboard for the Khmer script and published a weighty two-volume

32. Biographical materials on these men were kindly provided to me by Steve Heder.
33. He died in 1950, in a grenade attack on the Democratic Party headquarters organized by an unknown, but probably princely, hand.

Pheasa Khmer [The Khmer Language], or as the misleading title-page of the 1967 edition has it, *La Langue Cambodgienne (Un Essai d'étude raisonné).*[34] But this text made its first appearance — volume 1 only — in 1947, when its author was Chairman of the Constituent Assembly in Phnom Penh, not in 1937, when he was vegetating in Battambang, when as yet no Khmer-speaking *lycéens* had been produced by the Lycée Sisowath, and when Indochina still had an ephemeral reality. By 1947, Khmer-speakers — at least those from 'Cambodge' — were no longer attending classes in Saigon or Hanoi. A new generation was coming on the scene for whom 'Indochine' was history and 'Vietnam' now a real and foreign country.

It is true that brutal invasions and occupations during the nineteenth century, ordered by the Nguyên dynasts in Hué, left bitter folk-memories among the Khmer, including those in that Cochin China fated to become part of Vietnam. But comparable bitternesses existed in the Netherlands Indies: Sundanese against Javanese; Batak against Minangkabau; Sasak against Balinese; Toraja against Buginese; Javanese against Ambonese, and so on. The so-called 'federalist policy' pursued between 1945 and 1948 by the formidable Lieutenant Governor-General Hubertus van Mook to out-flank the infant Indonesian Republic attempted precisely to exploit such bitternesses.[35] But in spite of a spate of ethnic rebellions in almost all parts of independent Indonesia between 1950 and 1964, 'Indonesia' survived. In part it survived because Batavia remained the educational apex to the end, but also because colonial administrative policy did not rusticate educated Sundanese to the 'Sundalands,' or Batak to their place of origin in the highlands of North Sumatra. Virtually all the major ethnolinguistic groups were, by the end of the colonial period, accustomed to the idea that there was an archipelagic stage on which they had parts to play. Thus, only one of the rebellions of 1950–64 had *separatist* ambitions; all the rest were competitive within a single Indonesian political system.[36]

34. Published in Phnom Penh by the Librairie Mitserei [Free Friends]. 'Misleading' because the entire text is in Khmer. Biographical details on Ieu Koeus, drawn from his 1964 cremation volume, were generously passed on to me by Steve Heder.

35. See Kahin, *Nationalism,* chapter 12; Anthony Reid, *The Indonesian National Revolution, 1945–50,* chapter 6; and Henri Alers, *Om een rode of groene Merdeka,* passim.

36. The exception was the abortive Republic of the South Moluccas. Christianized Ambonese had long been heavily recruited for the repressive colonial army. Many fought under van Mook against the new-born revolutionary Indonesian Republic; after Holland's recognition of Indonesian independence in 1950, they had some reason to expect an unpleasant future.

In addition, one can not ignore the curious accident that by the 1920s an 'Indonesian language' had come into self-conscious existence. How this accident came about is so instructive that it seems worth a brief digression. Earlier, mention was made of the fact that only to a limited and late extent were the Indies ruled through Dutch. How could it not be so, when the Dutch had begun their local conquests in the early seventeenth century, while Dutch-language instruction for *inlanders* was not seriously under-taken until the early twentieth? What happened instead was that by a slow, largely unplanned process, a strange language-of-state evolved on the basis of an ancient interinsular lingua franca.[37] Called *dienstmaleisch* (perhaps 'service-Malay' or 'administrative-Malay'), it belonged typologically with 'Ottoman' and that 'fiscal German' which emerged from the polyglot bar-racks of the Habsburg empire.[38] By the early nineteenth century it was solidly in place inside officialdom. When print-capitalism arrived on the scene in a sizeable way after mid-century, the language moved out into the marketplace and the media. Used at first mainly by Chinese and Eurasian newspapermen and printers, it was picked up by *inlanders* at the century's close. Quickly the *dienst* branch of its family tree was forgotten and replaced by a putative ancestor in the Riau Islands (of which the most important had – perhaps fortunately – since 1819 become British Singa-pore). By 1928, shaped by two generations of urban writers and readers, it was ready to be adopted by Young Indonesia as the national(-ist) language *bahasa Indonesia*. Since then, it has never looked back.

Yet, in the end, the Indonesian case, interesting as it is, should not mislead us into thinking that, if Holland had been a bigger power,[39] and had arrived in 1850 rather than 1600, the national language could not just

37. See the valuable account in John Hoffman, 'A Foreign Investment: Indies Malay to 1901,' *Indonesia*, 27 (April 1979), pp. 65–92.

38. The military 'constituted something like an *anational caste*, the members of which lived even in their private lives ordinarily distinct from their national environments and spoke very often a special language, the so-called *ärarisch deutsch* ("fiscal German"), as it was ironically named by the representatives of the literary German, meaning by it a strange linguistic mixture which does not take the rules of grammar very seriously.' Jászi, *The Dissolution*, p. 144. Author's emphases.

39. Not merely in the obvious senses. Because, in the eighteenth and nineteenth centuries, Holland had, for all intents and purposes, only one colony, and a huge, profitable one at that, it was quite practical to train its functionaries in a (single) non-European *diensttaal*. Over time, special schools and faculties grew up in the metropole to prepare future functionaries linguistically. For multi-continental empires like the British, no single locally-based *diensttaal* would have sufficed.

as well have been Dutch. Nothing suggests that Ghanaian nationalism is any less real than Indonesian simply because its national language is English rather than Ashanti. It is always a mistake to treat languages in the way that certain nationalist ideologues treat them − as *emblems* of nation-ness, like flags, costumes, folk-dances, and the rest. Much the most important thing about language is its capacity for generating imagined communities, building in effect *particular solidarities.* After all, imperial languages are still *vernaculars,* and thus particular vernaculars among many. If radical Mozambique speaks Portuguese, the significance of this is that Portuguese is the medium through which Mozambique is imagined (and at the same time limits its stretch into Tanzania and Zambia). Seen from this perspective the use of Portuguese in Mozambique (or English in India) is basically no different than the use of English in Australia or Portuguese in Brazil. Language is not an instrument of exclusion: in principle, anyone can learn any language. On the contrary, it is fundamentally inclusive, limited only by the fatality of Babel: no one lives long enough to learn *all* languages. Print-language is what invents nationalism, not *a* particular language per se.[40] The only question-mark standing over languages like Portuguese in Mozambique and English in India is whether the administrative and educational systems, particularly the latter, can generate a politically sufficient diffusion of bilingualism. Thirty years ago, almost no Indonesian spoke *bahasa Indonesia* as his or her mother-tongue; virtually everyone had their own 'ethnic' language and some, especially people in the nationalist movement, *bahasa Indonesia/dienstmaleisch* as well. Today there are perhaps millions of young Indonesians, from dozens of ethnolinguistic backgrounds, who speak Indonesian as their mother-tongue.

It is not clear yet whether thirty years from now there will be a genera-

40. Marr's account of language-development in eastern Indochina is very revealing on this point. He notes that as late as c. 1910 'most educated Vietnamese assumed that Chinese or French, or both, were essential modes of "higher" communication.' (*Vietnamese Tradition,* p. 137). After 1920, however, and partly as a result of state promotion of the phonetic *quốc ngữ* script, things changed quickly. By then 'the belief was growing that spoken Vietnamese was an important and perhaps [sic] essential component of national identity. Even intellectuals more at home in French than in their mother tongue came to appreciate the significance of the fact that at least 85% of their fellow-countrymen spoke the same language.' (p. 138) They were by then fully aware of the role of mass literacy in advancing the nation-states of Europe and Japan. Yet Marr also shows that for a long time there was no clear correlation between language-preference and political stance: 'Upholding the Vietnamese mother tongue was not inherently patriotic, any more than promoting the French language was inherently collaborationist.' (p. 150).

tion of Mozambiquians who speak only Mozambique-Portuguese. But, in this late twentieth century, it is not necessarily the case that the emergence of such a generation is a *sine qua non* for Mozambiquian national solidarity. In the first place, advances in communications technology, especially radio and television, give print allies unavailable a century ago. Multilingual broadcasting can conjure up the imagined community to illiterates and populations with different mother-tongues. (Here there are resemblances to the conjuring up of mediaeval Christendom through visual representations and bilingual literati.) In the second place, twentieth-century nationalisms have, as I have been arguing, a profoundly modular character. They can, and do, draw on more than a century and a half of human experience and three earlier models of nationalism. Nationalist leaders are thus in a position consciously to deploy civil and military educational systems modelled on official nationalism's; elections, party organizations, and cultural celebrations modelled on the popular nationalisms of nineteenth-century Europe; and the citizen-republican idea brought into the world by the Americas. Above all, the very idea of 'nation' is now nestled firmly in virtually all print-languages; and nation-ness is virtually inseparable from political consciousness.

In a world in which the national state is the overwhelming norm, all of this means that nations can now be imagined without linguistic communality — not in the naive spirit of *nosotros los Americanos,* but out of a general awareness of what modern history has demonstrated to be possible.[41] It seems fitting, in this context, to conclude this chapter by returning to Europe and considering briefly that nation whose linguistic diversity has so often been used as a cudgel to club proponents of language-based theories of nationalism.

In 1891, amidst novel jubilees marking the 600th anniversary of the Confederacy of Schwyz, Obwalden, and Nidwalden, the Swiss state 'decided on' 1291 as the date of the 'founding' of Switzerland.[42] Such a decision, waiting 600 years to be made, has its diverting aspects, and suggests already that modernity rather than antiquity characterizes Swiss nationalism. Indeed, Hughes goes so far as to argue that the 1891 jubilees

41. I say 'can' because there are obviously plenty of cases where the possibility has been, and is being, rejected. In such cases, for example Old Pakistan, the explanation is not ethno-cultural pluralism, but barred pilgrimages.

42. Christopher Hughes, *Switzerland*, p. 107. This excellent text, for which Seton-Watson rightly expresses his admiration, is the basis for the argument that follows.

124

mark the birth of this nationalism, commenting that 'in the first half of the nineteenth century . . . nationhood sat rather lightly on the shoulders of the cultivated middle classes: Mme. de Staël [1766–1817], Fuseli [1741–1825], Angelica Kauffmann [1741–1807], Sismondi [1773–1842], Benjamin Constant [1767–1830], are they all Swiss?'[43] If the implied answer is 'hardly,' its significance derives from the fact that all over the Europe surrounding Switzerland, the first half of the nineteenth century saw the burgeoning of vernacular nationalist movements in which 'cultivated middle classes' (as it were, philologists + capitalists) played central parts. Why then did nationalism come so late to Switzerland, and what consequences did that lateness have for its ultimate shaping (in particular, its contemporary multiplicity of 'national languages')?

Part of the answer lies in the youth of the Swiss state, which, Hughes dryly observes, is difficult to trace back beyond 1813–15 'without the aid of some prevarication.'[44] He reminds us that the first real Swiss citizenship, the introduction of direct (male) suffrage, and the ending of 'internal' tolls and customs areas were achievements of the Helvetic Republic forcibly brought into being by the French occupation of 1798. Only in 1803 did the state include significant numbers of Italian-speakers, with the acquisition of Ticino. Only in 1815 did it gain the populous French-speaking areas of Valais, Geneva, and Neuchâtel from a vengefully anti-French Holy Alliance – in exchange for neutrality and a highly conservative constitution.[45] In effect, today's multilingual Switzerland is a product of the early nineteenth century.[46]

A second factor was the country's backwardness (which, combined with its forbidding topography and lack of exploitable resources, helped to keep it from absorption by more powerful neighbours). Today it may be difficult to remember that until World War II Switzerland was a poor country, with a standard of living half that of England's, and an overwhelmingly *rural*

43. Ibid., p. 218. The dates are my interpolations.
44. Ibid., p. 85.
45. Plus Aargau, St. Gallen and Grisons. This last is of special interest since today it is the surviving home of Romansch, the most echt-Swiss of the country's national languages – a status it achieved, however, only in 1937! Ibid., pp. 59 and 85.
46. We might note in passing that Mme. de Staël barely survived long enough to see its birth. Besides, her family, like that of Sismondi, came from Geneva, which was an independent statelet outside 'Switzerland' until 1815. Small wonder that Swiss nationhood rested 'rather lightly' on their shoulders.

country. In 1850, barely 6% of the population lived in minimally urban areas, and as late as 1920 the figure had risen only to 27.6%.[47] Throughout the nineteenth century, then, the bulk of the population was an immobile (except for the age-old export of hardy youths as mercenaries and Papal Guards) peasantry. The country's backwardness was not merely economic, it was also political and cultural. 'Old Switzerland,' the area of which did not change between 1515 and 1803, and most of whose inhabitants spoke one or other of numerous German patois, was ruled by a loose coalition of cantonal aristocratic oligarchies. 'The secret of the long duration of the Confederacy was its double nature. Against outside enemies it produced a sufficient unity of peoples. Against internal rebellion, it produced a sufficient unity of oligarchies. If peasants rebelled, as they did three times or so in every century, then differences would be put aside and the *governments* of other cantons would lend their assistance, mediating often, but not always, in favour of their fellow-ruler.'[48] Except for the absence of monarchical institutions, the picture is not much different from that of the innumerable petty principalities within the Holy Roman Empire, of which Liechtenstein, on Switzerland's eastern border, is a last odd relic.[49]

It is instructive that as late as 1848, almost two generations after the Swiss state came into being, ancient religious cleavages were much more politically salient than linguistic ones. Remarkably enough, in territories unalterably-denoted Catholic Protestantism was *unlawful,* and in those so-denoted Protestant Catholicism was illegal; and these laws were strictly enforced. (Language was a matter of personal choice and convenience). Only after 1848, in the backwash of Europe-wide revolutionary upheavals and the general spread of vernacularizing national movements, did language take religion's place, and the country become segmented into unalterably-denoted linguistic zones. (Religion now became a matter of personal choice).[50]

Finally, the persistence — in such a small country — of a large variety of sometimes mutually-unintelligible German idiolects suggests the late arrival of print-capitalism and standardized modern education to much of Swiss peasant society. Thus *Hochsprache* (print-German) has had, until rather recently, the language-of-state status of *ärarisch deutsch* and *dienst-*

47. Ibid., pp. 173 and 274. Any nineteenth-century 'cultivated middle class' had to be very small.

48. Ibid., p. 86. Emphasis added.

49. An absence of monarchies also characterized the Hanseatic League, a loose political coalition to which it would be problematic to attribute either statehood or nationhood.

50. Ibid., p. 274.

maleisch. Furthermore, Hughes remarks that today 'higher' officials are expected to have a working knowledge of two federal languages, implying that the same competence is not expected of their subordinates. Indirectly, a similar point is made by the Federal Directive of 1950 which insists that '*Educated* German Swiss are certainly able to work in French, as are *educated* Italian Swiss.'[51] We have, in effect, a situation which at bottom is not too different from Mozambique's – a bilingual political class ensconced over a variety of monolingual populations, with only this dissimilarity: the 'second language' is that of a powerful neighbour rather than of a former colonial ruler.

Nonetheless, in view of the fact that in 1910 the maternal language of almost 73% of the population was German, 22% French, 4% Italian, and 1% Romansch (these proportions have scarcely varied over the intervening decades), it is perhaps surprising that in the second half of the nineteenth century – era of official nationalisms – Germanification was not attempted. Certainly up to 1914 strong pro-German sympathies existed. Between Germany and German Switzerland borders were porous in the extreme. Trade and investment, as well as aristocrats and professionals, moved back and forth quite freely. But Switzerland also abutted on two other major European powers, France and Italy, and the political risks of Germanizing were plain. Legal parity between German, French, and Italian was thus the obverse side of the coin of Swiss neutrality.[52]

All of the preceding evidence indicates that Swiss nationalism is best understood as part of the 'last wave'. If Hughes is right in dating its birth to 1891, it is not much more than a decade older than Burmese or Indonesian nationalism. In other words, it arose in that period of world history in which the nation was becoming an international norm, and in which it was possible to 'model' nation-ness in a much more complex way than hitherto. If the conservative political, and backward socio-economic, structure of Switzerland 'delayed' the rise of nationalism,[53] the fact that its pre-modern political institutions were non-dynastic and non-monarchical helped to prevent the excesses of official nationalism (contrast the case of Siam discussed in Chapter 6). Finally, as in the case of the Southeast Asian

51. Ibid., pp. 59–60 Emphases added.
52. Romansch's elevation in 1937 scarcely disguised the original calculation.
53. The social structure of Hungary was also backward, but Magyar aristocrats sat inside a huge polyethnic dynastic empire, in which their putative language-group formed merely a minority, albeit a very important one. Small, republican Switzerland's aristocratic oligarchy was never threatened in the same way.

examples, the appearance of Swiss nationalism on the eve of the communications revolution of the twentieth century made it possible and practical to 'represent' the imagined community in ways that did not require linguistic uniformity.

In conclusion, it may be worth restating the general argument of this chapter. The 'last wave' of nationalisms, most of them in the colonial territories of Asia and Africa, was in its origins a response to the new-style global imperialism made possible by the achievements of industrial capitalism. As Marx put it in his inimitable way: 'The need of a constantly expanding market for its products chases the bourgeoisie over the whole face of the globe.'[54] But capitalism had also, not least by its dissemination of print, helped to create popular, vernacular-based nationalisms in Europe, which to different degrees undermined the age-old dynastic principle, and egged into self-naturalization every dynasty positioned to do so. Official nationalism – weld of the new national and old dynastic principles (the *British* Empire) – led in turn to what, for convenience, one can call 'Russification' in the extra-European colonies. This ideological tendency meshed neatly with practical exigencies. The late-nineteenth-century empires were too large and too far-flung to be ruled by a handful of nationals. Moreover, in tandem with capitalism the state was rapidly multiplying its functions, in both the metropoles and the colonies. Combined, these forces generated 'Russifying' school-systems intended in part to produce the required subordinate cadres for state and corporate bureaucracies. These school-systems, centralized and standardized, created quite new pilgrimages which typically had their Romes in the various colonial capitals, for the nations hidden at the core of the empires would permit no more inward ascension. Usually, but by no means always, these educational pilgrimages were paralleled, or replicated, in the administrative sphere. The interlock between particular educational and administrative pilgrimages provided the territorial base for new 'imagined communities' in which 'natives' could come to see themselves as 'nationals'. The expansion of the colonial state which, so to speak, invited 'natives' into schools and offices, and of colonial capitalism which, as it were, excluded them from boardrooms, meant that to an unprecedented extent the key early spokesmen for colonial nationalism were lonely, bilingual intelligentsias unattached to sturdy local bourgeoisies.

54. Marx and Engels, *The Communist Manifesto*, p. 37. Who but Marx would have described this world-transforming class as being 'chased'?

As bilingual intelligentsias, however, and above all as early-twentieth-century intelligentsias, they had access, inside the classroom and outside, to models of nation, nation-ness, and nationalism distilled from the turbulent, chaotic experiences of more than a century of American and European history. These models, in turn, helped to give shape to a thousand inchoate dreams. In varying combinations, the lessons of creole, vernacular and official nationalism were copied, adapted, and improved upon. Finally, as with increasing speed capitalism transformed the means of physical and intellectual communication, the intelligentsias found ways to bypass print in propagating the imagined community, not merely to illiterate masses, but even to literate masses *reading* different languages.

8

Patriotism and Racism

In the preceding chapters I have tried to delineate the processes by which the nation came to be imagined, and, once imagined, modelled, adapted and transformed. Such an analysis has necessarily been concerned primarily with social change and different forms of consciousness. But it is doubtful whether either social change or transformed consciousnesses, in themselves, do much to explain the *attachment* that peoples feel for the inventions of their imaginations – or, to revive a question raised at the beginning of this text – why peoples are ready to die for these inventions.

In an age when it is so common for progressive, cosmopolitan intellectuals (particularly in Europe?) to insist on the near-pathological character of nationalism, its roots in fear and hatred of the Other, and its affinities with racism,[1] it is useful to remind ourselves that nations inspire love, and often profoundly self-sacrificing love. The cultural products of nationalism – poetry, prose fiction, music, plastic arts – show this love very clearly in thousands of different forms and styles. On the other hand, how truly rare it is to find *analogous* nationalist products expressing fear and loathing.[2] Even in the case of colonized peoples, who have every reason to feel hatred for their imperialist rulers, it is astonishing how insignificant the element of hatred is in these expressions of national feeling. Here, for example, are

---

1. Cf. the passage in Nairn's *Break-up of Britain*, pp. 14–15 above, and Hobsbawm's somewhat Biedermeier dictum: 'the basic fact [is] that Marxists as such are not nationalists.' 'Some Reflections,' p. 10.

2. Can the reader think immediately of even three Hymns of Hate? The second stanza of God Save the Queen/King is worded instructively: O Lord our God, arise/Scatter her/his enemies,/And make them fall;/Confound their knavish tricks;/On Thee our hopes we fix;/God save us all. Notice that these enemies have no identity and could as well be Englishmen as anyone else since they are 'her/his' enemies *not* 'ours.' The entire anthem is a paean to monarchy, not to the/a nation – which is not once mentioned.

the first and last stanzas of *Último Adiós*, the famous poem written by Rizal as he awaited execution at the hands of Spanish imperialism:[3]

1. Adiós, Patria adorada, región del sol querida,
   Perla del mar de Oriente, nuestro perdido edén,
   A darte voy, alegre, la triste mustia vida;
   Y fuera más brillante, más fresca, más florida,
   También por ti la diera, la diera por tu bien. . .

12. Entonces nada importa me pongas en olvido:
    Tu atmósfera, tu espacio, tus valles cruzaré;
    Vibrante y limpia nota seré par to oído;
    Aroma, luz, colores, rumor, canto, gemido,
    Constante repitiendo le esencia de mi fe.

13. Mi Patria idolatrada, dolor de mis dolores,
    Querida Filipinas, oye el postrer adiós.
    Ahí, te dejo todo: mis padres, mis amores.
    Voy donde no hay esclavos, verdugos ni opresores;
    Donde la fe no mata, donde el que reina es Dios.

14. Adiós, padres y hermanos, trozos del alma mía,
    Amigos de la infancia, en el perdido hogar;
    Dad gracias, que descanso del fatigoso día;
    Adiós, dulce extranjera, mi amiga, mi alegría;
    Adiós, queridos séres. Morir es descansar.

Or, in the translation of Trinidad T. Subido:

1. Farewell, dear Land, beloved of the sun,
   Pearl of the Orient seas, lost Paradise!
   Gladly, I will to you this life undone;
   Were it a fairer, fresher, fuller one,
   I'd cede it still, your weal to realize. . .

12. What matters then that you forget me, when
    I might explore your ev'ry dear retreat?
    Be as a note, pulsing and pure; and then,
    Be scent, light, tone; be song or sign, again;
    And through it all, my theme of faith, repeat.

3. Jaime C. de Veyra, *El 'Último Adiós' de Rizal: estudio crítico-expositivo*, pp. 89–90, and 101–102 (the translation).

13. Land I enshrine, list to my last farewell!
    Philippines, Love, of pains my pain extreme,
    I leave you all, all whom I love so well,
    To go where neither slaves nor tyrants dwell,
    Where Faith kills not, and where God reigns supreme.

14. Farewell to all my soul does comprehend —
    O kith and kin in my home dispossessed;
    Give thanks my day oppressive is at end;
    Farewell, sweet stranger, my delight and friend;
    Farewell, dear ones. To die is but to rest.

Notice not only that the nationality of the 'tyrants' goes unmentioned, but that Rizal's passionate patriotism is expressed superbly in 'their' language.[4]

Something of the nature of this political love can be deciphered from the ways in which languages describe its object: either in the vocabulary of kinship (motherland, *Vaterland, patria*) or that of home (*heimat* or *tanah air* [earth and water, the phrase for the Indonesians' native archipelago]). Both idioms denote something to which one is naturally tied. As we have seen earlier, in everything 'natural' there is always something unchosen. In this way, nation-ness is assimilated to skin-colour, gender, parentage, and birth-era — all those things one can not help. And in these 'natural ties' one senses what one might call 'the beauty of *gemeinschaft.*' To put it another way, precisely because such ties are not chosen, they have about them a halo of disinterestedness.

While it is true that in the past two decades the idea of the family-as-articulated-power-structure has been much written about, such a conception is certainly foreign to the overwhelming bulk of mankind. Rather, the family has traditionally been conceived as the domain of disinterested love and solidarity. So too, if historians, diplomats, politicians, and social scientists are quite at ease with the idea of 'national interest,' for most ordinary people of whatever class the whole point of the nation is that it is interestless. Just for that reason, it can ask for sacrifices.

As noted earlier, the great wars of this century are extraordinary not so much in the unprecedented scale on which they permitted people to kill, as in the colossal numbers persuaded to lay down their lives. Is it not certain that the numbers of those killed vastly exceeded those who killed? The idea

4. It was, however, quickly translated into Tagalog by the great Filipino revolutionary Andrés Bonifacio. His version is given in ibid., pp. 107–109.

of the ultimate sacrifice comes only with an idea of purity, through fatality.

Dying for one's country, which usually one does not choose, assumes a moral grandeur which dying for the Labour Party, the American Medical Association, or perhaps even Amnesty International can not rival, for these are all bodies one can join or leave at easy will. Dying for the revolution also draws its grandeur from the degree to which it is felt to be something fundamentally pure. (If people imagined the proletariat *merely* as a group in hot pursuit of refrigerators, holidays, or power, how far would they, including members of the proletariat, be willing to die for it?)[5] Ironically enough, it may be that to the extent that Marxist interpretations of history are felt (rather than intellected) as representations of ineluctable necessity, they also acquire an aura of purity and disinterestedness.

Here we may usefully return once more to language. First, one notes the primordialness of languages, even those known to be modern. No one can give the date for the birth of any language. Each looms up imperceptibly out of a horizonless past. (Insofar as *homo sapiens* is *homo dicens*, it can seem difficult to imagine an origin of language newer than the species itself.) Languages thus appear rooted beyond almost anything else in contemporary societies. At the same time, nothing connects us affectively to the dead more than language. If English-speakers hear the words 'Earth to earth, ashes to ashes, dust to dust' – created almost four and a half centuries ago – they get a ghostly intimation of simultaneity across homogenous, empty time. The weight of the words derives only in part from their solemn meaning; it comes also from an as-it-were ancestral 'Englishness'.

Second, there is a special kind of contemporaneous community which language alone suggests – above all in the form of poetry and songs. Take national anthems, for example, sung on national holidays. No matter how banal the words and mediocre the tunes, there is in this singing an experience of simultaneity. At precisely such moments, people wholly unknown to each other utter the same verses to the same melody. The image: unisonance.[6] Singing the Marseillaise, Waltzing Matilda, and Indonesia Raya provide occasions for unisonality, for the echoed physical realization of the imagined community. (So does listening to [and maybe silently

---

5. This formulation should not at all be taken to mean that revolutionary movements do not pursue material objectives. But these objectives are envisioned, not as a congeries of individual acquisitions, but as the conditions of Rousseau's shared *bonheur*.

6. Contrast this *a capella* chorus with the language of everyday life, which is typically experienced decani/cantoris-fashion as dialogue and exchange.

chiming in with] the recitation of ceremonial poetry, such a sections of *The Book of Common Prayer*.) How selfless this unisonance feels! If we are aware that others are singing these songs precisely when and as we are, we have no idea who they may be, or even where, out of earshot, they are singing. Nothing connects us all but imagined sound.

Yet such choruses are joinable in time. If I am a Lett, my daughter may be an Australian. The son of an Italian immigrant to New York will find ancestors in the Pilgrim Fathers. If nationalness has about it an aura of fatality, it is nonetheless a fatality embedded in *history*. Here San Martín's edict baptizing Quechua-speaking Indians as 'Peruvians' – a movement that has affinities with religious conversion – is exemplary. For it shows that from the start the nation was conceived in language, not in blood, and that one could be 'invited into' the imagined community. Thus today, even the most insular nations accept the principle of *naturalization* (wonderful word!), no matter how difficult in practice they may make it.

Seen as both a *historical* fatality and as a community imagined through language, the nation presents itself as simultaneously open and closed. This paradox is well illustrated in the shifting rhythms of these famous lines on the death of John Moore during the battle of Coruña:[7]

1. Not a drum was heard, not a funeral note,
     As his corse to the rampart we hurried;
   Not a soldier discharged his farewell shot
       O'er the grave where our hero we buried.

2. We buried him darkly at dead of night,
     The sods with our bayonets turning;
   By the struggling moonbeams' misty light,
     And the lantern dimly burning.

3. No useless coffin enclosed his breast,
     Not in sheet or in shroud we wound him;
   But he lay like a warrior taking his rest,
     With his martial cloak around him. . .

5. We thought, as we hollowed his narrow bed,
     And smoothed down his lonely pillow,
   That the foe and the stranger would tread o'er his head,
     And we far away on the billow. . .

7. 'The Burial of Sir John Moore,' in *The Poems of Charles Wolfe*, pp. 1–2.

134

8. Slowly and sadly we laid him down,
    From the field of his fame fresh and gory;
    We carved not a line, and we raised not a stone —
    But we left him alone with his glory!

The lines celebrate a heroic memory with a beauty inseparable from the English language — one untranslatable, audible only to its speakers and readers. Yet both Moore and his eulogist were Irishmen. And there is no reason why a descendant of Moore's French or Spanish 'foes' can not fully hear the poem's resonance: English, like any other language, is always open to new speakers, listeners, and readers.

Listen to Thomas Browne, encompassing in a pair of sentences the length and breadth of man's history:[8]

> Even the old ambitions had the advantage of ours, in the attempts of their vainglories, who acting early and before the probable Meridian of time, have by this time found great accomplishment of their designs, whereby the ancient Heroes have already out-lasted their Monuments, and Mechanicall preservations. But in this latter Scene of time we cannot expect such Mummies unto our memories, when ambition may fear the Prophecy of Elias, and Charles the Fifth can never hope to live within two Methusela's of Hector.

Here ancient Egypt, Greece, and Judaea are united with the Holy Roman Empire, but their unification across thousands of years and thousands of miles is accomplished within the particularity of Browne's seventeenth-century English prose.[9] The passage can, of course, up to a point be translated. But the eerie splendour of 'probable Meridian of time,' 'Mechanicall preservations,' 'such Mummies unto our memories,' and 'two Methusela's of Hector' can bring goose-flesh to the napes only of English-readers.

On this page, it opens itself wide to the reader. On the other hand, the no less eerie splendour of the final lines of 'Yang Sudah Hilang' by the great Indonesian author Pramoedya Ananta Toer:[10]

> Suara itu hanya terdengar beberapa detik saja dalam hidup. Getarannya sebentar berdengung, takkan terulangi lagi. Tapi seperti juga halnya dengan

8. *Hydriotaphia, Urne-Buriall, or, A Discourse of the Sepulchrall Urnes lately found in Norfolk*, pp. 72–73. On 'the probable Meridian of time' compare Bishop Otto of Freising.
9. Yet 'England' goes unmentioned in this unification. We are reminded of those provincial newspapers which brought the whole world, through Spanish, into Caracas and Bogotá.
10. In *Tjerita dari Blora* [Tales from Blora], pp. 15–44, at p. 44.

kali Lusi yang abadi menggarisi kota Blora, dan seperti kali itu juga, suara yang tersimpan menggarisi kenangan dan ingatan itu mengalir juga – mengalir kemuaranya, kelaut yang tak bertepi. Dan tak seorangpun tahu kapan laut itu akan kering dan berhenti berdeburan.
Hilang.
Semua itu sudah hilang dari jangkauan panc[h]a-indera.

on the same print page, are most likely closed.[11]

If every language is acquirable, its acquisition requires a real portion of a person's life: each new conquest is measured against shortening days. What limits one's access to other languages is not their imperviousness but one's own mortality. Hence a certain privacy to all languages. French and American imperialists governed, exploited, and killed Vietnamese over many years. But whatever else they made off with, the Vietnamese language stayed put. Accordingly, only too often, a rage at Vietnamese 'inscrutability,' and that obscure despair which engenders the venomous argots of dying colonialisms: 'gooks,' *'ratons*,' etc.[12] (In the longer run, the only responses to the vast privacy of the language of the oppressed are retreat or further massacre.)

Such epithets are, in their inner form, characteristically racist, and decipherment of this form will serve to show why Nairn is basically mistaken in arguing that racism and anti-semitism derive from nationalism – and thus that 'seen in sufficient historical depth, facism tells us more about nationalism than any other episode.'[13] A word like 'slant,' for example, abbreviated from 'slant-eyed', does not simply express an ordinary political enmity. It *erases nation-ness* by reducing the adversary to his biological physiognomy.[14] It denies, by substituting for, 'Vietnamese,' just as *raton* denies, by substituting for, 'Algerian'. At the same time, it stirs 'Vietnamese' into a nameless sludge along with 'Korean,' 'Chinese,' 'Filipino,' and so on. The character of this vocabulary may become still more evident if it is contrasted with other Vietnam-War-period words like 'Charlie' and 'V.C.', or from an earlier era, 'Boches,' 'Huns,' 'Japs' and 'Frogs,' all of

11. Still, listen to them! I have adapted the original spelling to accord with current convention and to make the quotation completely phonetic.
12. The logic here is: 1. I will be dead before I have penetrated them. 2. My power is such that they have had to learn my language. 3. But this means that my privacy has been penetrated. Terming them 'gooks' is small revenge.
13. *The Break-up of Britain*, pp. 337 and 347.
14. Notice that there is no obvious, selfconscious antonym to 'slant.' 'Round'? 'Straight'? 'Oval'?

which apply only to *one* specific nationality, and thus concede, in hatred, the adversary's membership in a league of nations.[15]

The fact of the matter is that nationalism thinks in terms of historical destinies, while racism dreams of eternal contaminations, transmitted from the origins of time through an endless sequence of loathsome copulations: outside history. Niggers are, thanks to the invisible tar-brush, forever niggers; Jews, the seed of Abraham, forever Jews, no matter what passports they carry or what languages they speak and read. (Thus for the Nazi, the *Jewish* German was always an impostor.)[16]

The dreams of racism actually have their origin in ideologies of *class*, rather than in those of nation: above all in claims to divinity among rulers and to 'blue' or 'white' blood and 'breeding' among aristocracies.[17] No surprise then that the putative sire of modern racism should be, not some petty-bourgeois nationalist, but Joseph Arthur, Comte de Gobineau.[18] Nor that, on the whole, racism and anti-semitism manifest themselves, not across national boundaries, but within them. In other words, they justify not so much foreign wars as domestic repression and domination.[19]

Where racism developed outside Europe in the nineteenth century, it

15. Not only, in fact, in an earlier era. Nonetheless, there is a whiff of the antique-shop about these words of Debray: 'I can conceive of no hope for Europe save under the hegemony of a revolutionary France, firmly grasping the banner of independence. Sometimes I wonder if the whole "anti-Boche" mythology and our secular antagonism to Germany may not be one day indispensable for saving the revolution, or even our national-democratic inheritance.' 'Marxism and the National Question,' p. 41.

16. The significance of the emergence of Zionism and the birth of Israel is that the former marks the reimagining of an ancient religious community as a nation, down there among the other nations – while the latter charts an alchemic change from wandering devotee to local patriot.

17. 'From the side of the landed aristocracy came conceptions of inherent superiority in the ruling class, and a sensitivity to status, prominent traits well into the twentieth century. Fed by new sources, these conceptions could later be vulgarized [sic] and made appealing to the German population as a whole in doctrines of racial superiority.' Barrington Moore, Jr., *Social Origins of Dictatorship and Democracy*, p. 436.

18. Gobineau's dates are perfect. He was born in 1816, two years after the restoration of the Bourbons to the French throne. His diplomatic career, 1848–1877, blossomed under Louis Napoléon's Second Empire and the reactionary monarchist regime of Marie Edmé Patrice Maurice, Comte de MacMahon, former imperialist proconsul in Algiers. His *Essai sur l'Inégalité des Races Humaines* appeared in 1854 – should one say in response to the popular vernacular-nationalist insurrections of 1848?

19. South African racism has not, in the age of Vorster and Botha, stood in the way of amicable relations (however discreetly handled) with prominent black politicians in certain independent African states. If Jews suffer discrimination in the Soviet Union, that did not prevent respectful working relations between Brezhnev and Kissinger.

was always associated with European domination, for two converging reasons. First and most important was the rise of official nationalism and colonial 'Russification'. As has been repeatedly emphasized, official nationalism was typically a response on the part of threatened dynastic and aristocratic groups — upper *classes* — to popular vernacular nationalism. Colonial racism was a major element in that conception of 'Empire' which attempted to weld dynastic legitimacy and national community. It did so by generalizing a principle of innate, inherited superiority on which its own domestic position was (however shakily) based to the vastness of the overseas possessions, covertly (or not so covertly) conveying the idea that if, say, English lords were naturally superior to other Englishmen, no matter: these other Englishmen were no less superior to the subjected natives. Indeed one is tempted to argue that the existence of late colonial empires even served to *shore up* domestic aristocratic bastions, since they appeared to confirm on a global, modern stage antique conceptions of power and privilege.

It could do so with some effect because — and here is our second reason — the colonial empire, with its rapidly expanding bureaucratic apparatus and its 'Russifying' policies, permitted sizeable numbers of bourgeois and petty bourgeois to play aristocrat off centre court: i.e. anywhere in the empire except at home. In each colony one found this grimly amusing *tableau vivant*: the bourgeois gentilhomme speaking poetry against a backcloth of spacious mansions and gardens filled with mimosa and bougainvillea, and a large supporting cast of houseboys, grooms, gardeners, cooks, amahs, maids, washerwomen, and, above all, horses.[20] Even those who did not manage to live in this style, such as young bachelors, nonetheless had the grandly equivocal status of a French nobleman on the eve of a jacquerie:[21]

> In Moulmein, in lower Burma [this obscure town needs explaining to readers in the metropole], I was hated by large numbers of people — the only time in my life that I have been important enough for this to happen to me. I was sub-divisional police officer of the town.

This 'tropical Gothic' was made possible by the overwhelming power that high capitalism had given the metropole — a power so great that it

---

20. For a stunning collection of photographs of such tableaux vivants in the Netherlands Indies (and an elegantly ironical text), see 'E. Breton de Nijs,' *Tempo Doeloe*.

21. George Orwell, 'Shooting an Elephant,' in *The Orwell Reader*, p. 3. The words in square brackets are of course my interpolation.

could be kept, so to speak, in the wings. Nothing better illustrates capitalism in feudal-aristocratic drag than colonial militaries, which were notoriously distinct from those of the metropoles, often even in formal institutional terms.[22] Thus in Europe one had the 'First Army', recruited by conscription on a mass, citizen, metropolitan base; ideologically conceived as the defender of the *heimat*; dressed in practical, utilitarian khaki; armed with the latest affordable weapons; in peacetime isolated in barracks, in war stationed in trenches or behind heavy field-guns. Outside Europe one had the 'Second Army,' recruited (below the officer level) from local religious or ethnic minorities on a mercenary basis; ideologically conceived as an internal police force; dressed to kill in bed- or ballroom; armed with swords and obsolete industrial weapons; in peace on display, in war on horseback. If the Prussian General Staff, Europe's military teacher, stressed the anonymous solidarity of a professionalized corps, ballistics, railroads, engineering, strategic planning, and the like, the colonial army stressed glory, epaulettes, personal heroism, polo, and an archaizing courtliness among its officers. (It could afford to do so because the First Army and the Navy were there in the background.) This mentality survived a long time. In Tonkin, in 1894, Lyautey wrote:[23]

> Quel dommage de n'être pas venu ici dix ans plus tôt! Quelles carrières à y fonder et à y mener. Il n'y a pas ici un de ces petits lieutenants, chefs de poste et de reconnaissance, qui ne développe en 6 mois plus d'initiative, de volonté, d'endurance, de *personnalité*, qu'un officier *de* France en toute sa carrière.

In Tonkin, in 1951, Jean de Lattre de Tassigny, 'who liked officers who combined guts with "style," took an immediate liking to the dashing cavalryman [Colonel de Castries] with his bright-red Spahi cap and scarf, his magnificent riding-crop, and his combination of easy-going manners and *ducal* mien, which made him as irresistible to women in Indochina in the 1950's as he had been to Parisiennes of the 1930's.'[24]

22. The KNIL (Koninklijk Nederlandsch-Indisch Leger) was quite separate from the KL (Koninklijk Leger) in Holland. The Légion Étrangère was almost from the start legally prohibited from operations on continental French soil.

23. *Lettres du Tonkin et de Madagascar (1894–1899)*, p. 84. Letter of December 22, 1894, from Hanoi. Emphases added.

24. Bernard B. Fall, *Hell is a Very Small Place: The Siege of Dien Bien Phu*, p. 56. One can imagine the shudder of Clausewitz's ghost. [Spahi, derived like Sepoy from the Ottoman Sipahi, meant mercenary irregular cavalrymen of the 'Second Army' in Algeria.] It is true that the France of Lyautey and de Lattre was a Republican France. However, the often talkative Grande Muette had since the start of the Third Republic been an asylum for aristocrats

Another instructive indication of the aristocratic or pseudo-aristocratic derivation of colonial racism was the typical 'solidarity among whites,' which linked colonial rulers from different national metropoles, whatever their internal rivalries and conflicts. This solidarity, in its curious trans-state character, reminds one instantly of the class solidarity of Europe's nineteenth-century aristocracies, mediated through each other's hunting-lodges, spas, and ballrooms; and of that brotherhood of 'officers and gentlemen,' which in the Geneva convention guaranteeing privileged treatment to captured enemy *officers*, as opposed to partisans or civilians, has an agreeably twentieth-century expression.

The argument adumbrated thus far can also be pursued from the side of colonial populations. For, the pronouncements of certain colonial ideologues aside, it is remarkable how little that dubious entity known as 'reverse racism' manifested itself in the anticolonial movements. In this matter it is easy to be deceived by language. There is, for example, a sense in which the Javanese word *londo* (derived from Hollander or Nederlander) meant not only 'Dutch' but 'whites.' But the derivation itself shows that, for Javanese peasants, who scarcely ever encountered any 'whites' but Dutch, the two meanings effectively overlapped. Similarly, in French colonial territories, '*les blancs*' meant rulers whose Frenchness was indistinguishable from their whiteness. In neither case, so far as I know, did *londo* or *blanc* either lose caste or breed derogatory secondary distinctions.[25]

---

increasingly excluded from power in all other important institutions of public life. By 1898, a full quarter of all Brigadier- and Major-Generals were aristocrats. Moreover, this aristocrat-dominated officer corps was crucial to nineteenth and twentieth-century French imperialism. 'The rigorous control imposed on the army in the *métropole* never extended fully to *la France d'outre-mer*. The extension of the French Empire in the nineteenth century was partially the result of uncontrolled initiative on the part of colonial military commanders. French West Africa, largely the creation of General Faidherbe, and the French Congo as well, owed most of their expansion to independent military forays into the hinterland. Military officers were also responsible for the *faits accomplis* which led to a French protectorate in Tahiti in 1842, and, to a lesser extent, to the French occupation of Tonkin in Indochina in the 1880's. . . In 1897 Galliéni summarily abolished the monarchy in Madagascar and deported the Queen, all without consulting the French government, which later accepted the *fait accompli*. . .' John S. Ambler, *The French Army in Politics, 1945–1962*, pp. 10–11 and 22.

25. I have never heard of an abusive argot word in Indonesian or Javanese for either 'Dutch' or 'white.' Compare the Anglo-Saxon treasury: niggers, wops, kikes, gooks, slants, fuzzywuz-zies, and a hundred more. It is possible that this innocence of racist argots is true primarily of colonized populations. Blacks in America – and surely elsewhere – have developed a varied counter-vocabulary (honkies, ofays, etc.).

On the contrary, the spirit of anticolonial nationalism is that of the heart-rending Constitution of Makario Sakay's short-lived Republic of Katalugan (1902), which said, among other things:[26]

> No Tagalog, born in this Tagalog archipelago, shall exalt any person above the rest because of his race or the colour of his skin; fair, dark, rich, poor, educated and ignorant — all are completely equal, and should be in one *loób* [inward spirit]. There may be differences in education, wealth, or appearance, but never in essential nature (*pagkatao*) and ability to serve a cause.

One can find without difficulty analogies on the other side of the globe. Spanish-speaking mestizo Mexicans trace their ancestries, not to Castilian conquistadors, but to half-obliterated Aztecs, Mayans, Toltecs and Zapotecs. Uruguayan revolutionary patriots, creoles themselves, took up the name of Tupac Amarú, the last great indigenous rebel against creole oppression, who died under unspeakable tortures in 1781.

It may appear paradoxical that the objects of all these attachments are 'imagined' — anonymous, faceless fellow-Tagalogs, exterminated tribes, Mother Russia, or the *tanah air*. But *amor patriae* does not differ in this respect from the other affections, in which there is always an element of fond imagining. (This is why looking at the photo-albums of strangers' weddings is like studying the archaeologist's groundplan of the Hanging Gardens of Babylon.) What the eye is to the lover — that particular, ordinary eye he or she is born with — language — whatever language history has made his or her mother-tongue — is to the patriot. Through that language, encountered at mother's knee and parted with only at the grave, pasts are restored, fellowships are imagined, and futures dreamed.

---

26. As cited in Reynaldo Ileto's masterly *Pasyon and Revolution: Popular Movements in the Philippines, 1840–1910*, p. 218. Sakay's rebel republic lasted until 1907, when he was captured and executed by the Americans. Understanding the first sentence requires remembering that three centuries of Spanish rule had produced a sizeable mestizo population in the islands.

9

The Angel of History

We began this brief study with the recent wars between the Socialist Republic of Vietnam, Democratic Kampuchea, and the People's Republic of China; so it is only fitting to return finally to that point of departure. Does anything of what has meantime been said help to deepen our understanding of their outbreak?

In *The Break-up of Britain*, Tom Nairn has some valuable words on the relationship between the British political system and those of the rest of the modern world:[1]

> Alone, [the British system] represented a 'slow, conventional growth, not like the others, the product of deliberate *invention*, resulting from a theory.' Arriving later, those others 'attempted to sum up at a stroke the fruits of the experience of the state which had evolved its constitutionalism through several centuries' . . . Because it was first, the English – later British – experience remained distinct. Because they came second, into a world where the English Revolution had already succeeded and expanded, later bourgeois societies could not repeat this early development. Their *study and imitation engendered something substantially different*: the truly modern doctrine of the abstract or 'impersonal' state which, because of its abstract nature, could be imitated in subsequent history.
>
> This may of course be seen as the ordinary logic of developmental processes. It was an early specimen of what was later dignified with such titles as 'the law of uneven and combined development.' Actual repetition and imitation are scarcely ever possible, whether politically, economically, socially, or technologically, because the universe is already too much altered by the first cause one is copying.

1. At pp. 17–18. Emphases added. The inner quotation is taken from Charles Frederick Strong's *Modern Political Constitutions*, p. 28.

What Nairn says of the modern state is no less true of the twin conceptions of which our three embattled socialist countries are contemporary realizations: revolution and nationalism. It is perhaps too easy to forget that this pair, like capitalism and Marxism, are *inventions*, on which patents are impossible to preserve. They are there, so to speak, for the pirating. Out of these piracies and *only* out of them, comes this well-known anomaly: societies such as those of Cuba, Albania, and China, which, insofar as they are revolutionary-socialist, conceive of themselves as 'ahead' of those of France, Switzerland, and the United States, but which, insofar as they are characterized by low productivity, miserable living standards, and backward technology, are no less certainly understood as 'behind.' (Thus Chou En-lai's melancholy dream of catching up with capitalist Britain by the year 2000.)

As noted earlier, Hobsbawm was right to observe that 'the French Revolution was not made or led by a formed party or movement in the modern sense, nor by men attempting to carry out a systematic programme.' But, thanks to print-capitalism, the French experience was not merely ineradicable from human memory, it was also learnable-from. Out of almost a century of modular theorizing and practical experimentation came the Bolsheviks, who made the first successful 'planned' revolution (even if the success would not have been possible without Hindenburg's earlier triumphs at Tannenberg and the Masurian Lakes) and attempted to carry out a systematic programme (even if in practice improvisation was the order of the day). It also seems clear that *without* such plans and programmes a revolution in a realm barely entering the era of industrial capitalism was out of the question. The Bolshevik revolutionary model has been decisive for all twentieth-century revolutions because it made them imaginable in societies still more backward than All the Russias. (It opened the possibility of, so to speak, cutting history off at the pass.) The skilful early experimentations of Mao Tse-tung confirmed the utility of the model outside Europe. One can thus see a sort of culmination of the modular process in the case of Cambodia, where in 1962 less than 2.5% of the

---

2. According to the calculations of Edwin Wells, on the basis of Table 9 in Cambodge, Ministère du Plan et Institut National de la Statistique et des Recherches Economiques, *Résultats Finals du Recensement Général de la Population 1962*. Wells divides the rest of the working population as follows: government officials and new petty bourgeoisie, 8%; traditional petty bourgeoisie (traders, etc.), 7.5%; agricultural proletariat, 1.8%; peasants, 78.3%. There were less than 1,300 capitalists owning actual manufacturing enterprises.

two-and-a-half-million-strong adult work-force was 'working class,' and less than 0.5% 'capitalists.'[2]

In much the same way, since the end of the eighteenth century nationalism has undergone a process of modulation and adaptation, according to different eras, political regimes, economies and social structures. The 'imagined community' has, as a result, spread out to every conceivable contemporary society. If it permissible to use modern Cambodia to illustrate an extreme modular transfer of 'revolution,' it is perhaps equitable to use Vietnam to illustrate that of nationalism, by a brief excursus on the nation's name.

On his coronation in 1802, Gia-long wished to call his realm 'Nam Việt' and sent envoys to gain Peking's assent. The Manchu Son of Heaven, however, insisted that it be 'Việt Nam.' The reason for this inversion is as follows: 'Việt Nam' (or in Chinese Yüeh-nan) means, roughly 'to the south of Việt (Yüeh),' a realm conquered by the Han seventeen centuries earlier and reputed to cover today's Chinese provinces of Kwangtung and Kwangsi, as well as the Red River valley. Gia-long's 'Nam Việt,' however, meant 'Southern Việt/Yüeh,'" in effect a claim *to* the old realm. In the words of Alexander Woodside, 'the name "Vietnam" as a whole was hardly so well esteemed by Vietnamese rulers a century ago, emanating as it had from Peking, as it is in this century. An artificial appellation then, it was used extensively neither by the Chinese nor by the Vietnamese. The Chinese clung to the offensive T'ang word "Annam" . . . The Vietnamese court, on the other hand, privately invented another name for its kingdom in 1838–39 and did not bother to inform the Chinese. Its new name, Dại Nam, the "Great South" or "Imperial South," appeared with regularity on court documents and official historical compilations. But it has not survived to the present.'[3] This new name is interesting in two respects. First, it contains no 'Viet'-namese element. Second, its territorial reference seems purely relational – 'south' (of the Middle Kingdom).[4]

That today's Vietnamese proudly defend a Việt Nam scornfully invented by a nineteenth-century Manchu dynast reminds us of Renan's dictum that

---

3. *Vietnam and the Chinese Model*, pp. 120–21.
4. This is not altogether surprising. 'The Vietnamese bureaucrat looked Chinese; the Vietnamese peasant looked Southeast Asian. The bureaucrat had to write Chinese, wear Chinese-style gowns, live in a Chinese-style house, ride in a Chinese-style sedan chair, and even follow Chinese-style idiosyncracies of conspicuous consumption, like keeping a goldfish pond in his Southeast Asian garden.' Ibid., p. 199.

nations must have 'oublié bien des choses,' but also paradoxically, of the imaginative power of nationalism.

If one looks back at the Vietnam of the 1930s or the Cambodia of the 1960s, one finds, *mutatis mutandis*, many similarities: a huge, illiterate, exploited peasantry, a minuscule working class, a fragmentary bourgeoisie, and a tiny, divided intelligentsia.[5] No sober contemporary analyst, viewing these conditions objectively, would in either case have predicted the revolutions soon to follow, or their wrecked triumphs. (In fact, much the same could be said, and for much the same reasons, of the China of 1910.) What made them possible, in the end, was 'planning revolution' and 'imagining the nation.'[6]

The policies of the Pol Pot regime can only in a very limited sense be attributed to traditional Khmer culture or to its leaders' cruelty, paranoia, and megalomania. The Khmer have had their share of megalomaniac despots; some of these, however, were responsible for Angkor. Far more important are the models of what revolutions have, can, should, and should not do, drawn from France, the USSR, China, and Vietnam – and all the books written about them in French.[7]

Much the same is true of nationalism. Contemporary nationalism is the heir to two centuries of historic change. For all the reasons that I have attempted to sketch out, the legacies are truly Janus-headed. For the legators include not only San Martín and Garibaldi, but Uvarov and

5. According to the 1937 census, 93–95% of the Vietnamese population was still living in rural areas. No more than 10% of the population was functionally literate in any script. No more than 20,000 persons had completed upper primary (grade 7–10) schooling between 1920 and 1938. And what Vietnamese Marxists called the 'indigenous bourgeoisie' – described by Marr as mainly absentee landlords, combined with some entrepreneurs and a few higher officials – totalled about 10,500 families, or about 0.5% of the population. *Vietnamese Tradition*, 25–26, 34, and 37. Compare the data in note 2 above.

6. And, as in the case of the Bolsheviks, fortunate catastrophes: for China, Japan's massive invasion in 1937; for Vietnam, the smashing of the Maginot Line and her own brief occupation by the Japanese; for Cambodia, the massive overflow of the American war on Vietnam into her eastern territories after March 1970. In each case the existing *ancien régime*, whether Kuomintang, French colonial, or feudal-monarchist, was fatally undermined by extraneous forces.

7. One might suggest 'yes' to the *levée en masse* and the Terror, 'no' to Thermidor and Bonapartism, for France; 'yes' to War Communism, collectivization, and the Moscow Trials, 'no' to N.E.P. and de-Stalinization, for the Soviet Union; 'yes' to peasant guerrilla communism, the Great Leap Forward, and the Cultural Revolution, 'no' to the Lushan Plenum, for China; 'yes' to the August Revolution and the formal liquidation of the Indochinese Communist Party in 1945, 'no' to damaging concessions to 'senior' communist parties as exemplified in the Geneva Accords, for Vietnam.

Macaulay. As we have seen, 'official nationalism' was from the start a conscious, self-protective *policy*, intimately linked to the preservation of imperial-dynastic interests. But once 'out there for all to see,' it was as copyable as Prussia's early-nineteenth-century military reforms, and by the same variety of political and social systems. The one persistent feature of this style of nationalism was, and is, that it is *official* – i.e. something emanating from the state, and serving the interests of the state first and foremost.

Thus the model of official nationalism assumes its relevance above all at the moment when revolutionaries successfully take control of the state, and are for the first time in a position to use the power of the state in pursuit of their visions. The relevance is all the greater insofar as even the most determinedly radical revolutionaries always, to some degree, inherit the state from the fallen regime. Some of these legacies are symbolic, but not the less important for that. Despite Trotsky's unease, the capital of the USSR was moved back to the old Czarist capital of Moscow; and for over 65 years CPSU leaders have made policy in the Kremlin, ancient citadel of Czarist power – out of all possible sites in the socialist state's vast territories. Similarly, the PRC's capital is that of the Manchus (while Chiang Kai-shek had moved it to Nanking), and the CCP leaders congregate in the Forbidden City of the Sons of Heaven. In fact, there are very few, if any, socialist leaderships which have *not* clambered up into such worn, warm seats. At a less obvious level, successful revolutionaries also inherit the wiring of the old state: sometimes functionaries and informers, but always files, dossiers, archives, laws, financial records, censuses, maps, treaties, correspondence, memoranda, and so on. Like the complex electrical-system in any large mansion when the owner has fled, the state awaits the new owner's hand at the switch to be very much its old brilliant self again.

One should therefore not be much surprised if revolutionary *leaderships*, consciously or unconsciously, come to play lord of the manor. We are not thinking here simply of Djugashvili's self-identification with Ivan Groznii, or Mao's expressed admiration for the tyrant Ch'in Shih Huang-ti, or Josip Broz's revival of Ruritanian pomp and ceremony.[8] 'Official nationalism' enters post-revolutionary leadership styles in a much more subtle way. By this I mean that such leaderships come easily to adopt the putative

---

8. See the extraordinary account, by no means wholly polemical, in Milovan Djilas, *Tito: the Story from Inside*, chapter 4, especially pp. 133 ff.

nationalnost of the older dynasts *and* the dynastic state. In a striking retroactive movement, dynasts who knew nothing of 'China,' 'Yugoslavia,' 'Vietnam' or 'Cambodia' become nationals (even if not always 'deserving' nationals). Out of this accommodation comes invariably that 'state' Machiavellism which is so striking a feature of post-revolutionary regimes in contrast to revolutionary nationalist movements. The more the ancient dynastic state is naturalized, the more its antique finery can be wrapped around revolutionary shoulders. The image of Jayavarman VII's Angkor, emblazoned on the flag of Marxist Democratic Kampuchea (as on those of Lon Nol's puppet republic and of Sihanouk's monarchical Cambodge), is a rebus not of piety but of power.[9]

I emphasize *leaderships*, because it is leaderships, not people, who inherit old switchboards and palaces. No one imagines, I presume, that the broad masses of the Chinese people give a fig for what happens along the colonial border between Cambodia and Vietnam. Nor is it at all likely that Khmer and Vietnamese peasants wanted wars between their peoples, or were consulted in the matter. In a very real sense these were 'chancellory wars' in which popular nationalism was mobilized largely after the fact and always in a language of self-defence. (Hence the particularly low enthusiasm in China, where this language was least plausible, even under the neon-lit blazon of 'Soviet hegemonism'.)[10]

In all of this, China, Vietnam, and Cambodia are not in the least unique.[11] This is why there are small grounds for hope that the precedents they have set for inter-socialist wars will not be followed, or that the imagined community of the socialist nation will soon be remaindered. But nothing can be usefully done to limit or prevent such wars unless we abandon fictions like 'Marxists as such are not nationalists,' or 'nationalism

---

9. Obviously, the tendencies outlined above are by no means characteristic only of revolutionary Marxist regimes. The focus here is on such regimes both because of the historic Marxist commitment to proletarian internationalism and the destruction of feudal and capitalist states, and because of the new Indochina wars. For a decipherment of the archaizing iconography of the right-wing Suharto regime in Indonesia, see my 'Cartoons and Monuments: The Evolution of Political Communication under the New Order', in Jackson and Pye (eds), *Political Power and Communications in Indonesia*, pp. 282–321.

10. The difference between the inventions of 'official nationalism' and those of other types is usually that between lies and myths.

11. On the other hand, it is possible that at the end of this century historians may attribute 'official nationalist' excesses committed by post-revolutionary socialist regimes in no small part to the disjuncture between socialist model and agrarian reality.

is the pathology of modern developmental history,' and, instead, do our slow best to learn the real, and imagined, experience of the past. Of the Angel of History, Walter Benjamin wrote that:[12]

> His face is turned towards the past. Where we perceive a chain of events, he sees one single catastrophe which keeps piling wreckage upon wreckage and hurls it in front of his feet. The angel would like to stay, awaken the dead, and make whole what has been smashed. But a storm is blowing from Paradise; it has got caught in his wings with such violence that the angel can no longer close them. This storm irresistibly propels him into the future to which his back is turned, while the pile of debris before him grows skyward. This storm is what we call progress.

But this angel is immortal, and our faces are turned towards the obscurity ahead.

---

12. *Illuminations*, p. 259. The angel's eye is that of *Weekend's* back-turned moving camera, before which wreck after wreck looms up momentarily on an endless highway before vanishing over the horizon.

Bibliography

Alrs, Henri J. *Om een rode of groene Merdeka. Tien jaren binnenlandse politiek. Indonesië, 1943–53*. Eindhoven: Vulkaan. 1956.

Ambler, John Steward. *The French Army in Politics, 1945–1962*. Columbus: Ohio State University Press. 1966.

Anderson, Benedict R. O'Gorman. 'Cartoons and Mouments: The Evolution of Political Communication under the New Order.' In Karl D. Jackson and Lucian W. Pye. Eds. *Political Power and Communications in Indonesia*. Berkeley, Los Angeles and London: University of California Press. 1978. pp. 282–321.

— 'Studies of the Thai State: The State of Thai Studies.' In Eliezer B. Ayal. Ed. *The State of Thai Studies: Analyses of Knowledge, Approaches, and Prospects in Anthropology, Art History, Economics, History and Political Science*. Athens, Ohio: Ohio University, Center for International Studies, Southeast Asia Program. 1979. pp. 193–247.

Auerbach, Erich. *Mimesis. The Representation of Reality in Western Literature*. Trans. Willard Trask. Garden City, N.Y.: Doubleday Anchor. 1957.

Baltazar, Francisco. *Florante at Laura*. Manila: Florentino. 1973. Based on the original Ramirez and Giraudier imprint of 1861.

Barnett, Anthony. 'Inter-Communist Conflicts and Vietnam.' *Bulletin of Concerned Asian Scholars*, 11:4 (October–December 1979). pp. 2–9. (Reprinted from *Marxism Today*, August 1979).

Battye, Noel A. 'The Military, Government and Society in Siam, 1868–1910. Politics and Military Reform in the Reign of King Chulalongkorn.' Ph.D. thesis. Cornell University. 1974.

Benda, Harry J. and John A. Larkin. Eds. *The World of Southeast Asia: Selected Historical Readings*. New York: Harper and Row. 1967.

Benjamin, Walter. *Illuminations*. London: Fontana. 1973.

Bloch, Marc. *Feudal Society*. Trans. I. A. Manyon. Chicago: University of Chicago Press. 1961. 2 vols.

— *Les Rois Thaumaturges*. Strasbourg: Librairie Istra. 1924.

Boxer, Charles R. *The Portuguese Seaborne Empire, 1415–1825*. New York: Knopf. 1969.

Browne, Thomas. *Hydriotaphia, Urne-Buriall, or A Discourse of the Sepulchrall Urnes lately found in Norfolk*. London: Noel Douglas Replicas. 1927.

Cambodge. Ministère du Plan et Institut National de la Statistique et des Recherches Economiques. *Résultats Finals du Recensement Général de la Population, 1962*. Phnom Penh. 1966.

Chambert-Loir, Henri. 'Mas Marco Kartodikromo (c. 1890–1932) ou L'Education Politique.' In Pierre-Bernard Lafont and Denys Lombard. Eds. *Littératures contemporaines de l'asie du sud-est*. Paris: L'Asiathèque. 1974. pp. 203–214.

Craig, Albert M. *Chōshū in the Meiji Restoration*. Cambridge, Mass.: Harvard University Press. 1967.

Craig, Gordon A. *The Politics of the Prussian Army, 1640–1945*. New York and Oxford: Oxford University Press. 1956.

Debray, Régis. 'Marxism and the National Question.' *New Left Review*, 105 (September–October 1977). pp. 25–41.

Defoe, Daniel. *Selected Poetry and Prose of Daniel Defoe*. Ed. Michael F. Shugrue. New York: Holt, Rinehart and Winston. 1968.

Djilas, Milovan. *Tito, the Inside Story*. Trans. Vasilije Kojač and Richard Hayes. London: Weidenfeld and Nicholson. 1980.

Eisenstein, Elizabeth L. 'Some Conjectures about the Impact of Printing on Western Society and Thought: A Preliminary Report.' *Journal of Modern History*. 40:1 (March 1968). pp. 1–56.

Fall, Bernard B. *Hell is a Very Small Place. The Siege of Dien Bien Phu*. New York: Vintage. 1968.

Febvre, Lucien, and Henri-Jean Martin. *The Coming of the Book. The Impact of Printing, 1450–1800*. London: New Left Books. 1976. [Translation of *L'Apparition du Livre*. Paris: Albin Michel. 1958]

Fields, Rona M. *The Portuguese Revolution and the Armed Forces Movement*. New York, Washington and London: Praeger. 1975.

Franco, Jean. *An Introduction to Spanish-American Literature*. Cambridge: Cambridge University Press. 1969.

Gellner, Ernest. *Thought and Change*. London: Weidenfeld and Nicholson. 1964.

Gilmore, Robert L. *Caudillism and Militarism in Venezuela, 1810–1910*. Athens, Ohio: Ohio University Press. 1964.

Greene, Stephen. 'Thai Government and Administration in the Reign of Rama VI (1910–1925).' Ph.D. thesis. University of London. 1971.

Heder, Stephen P. 'The Kampuchean-Vietnamese Conflict.' In David W. P. Elliott. Ed. *The Third Indochina Conflict*. Boulder: Westview Press. 1981. pp. 21–67. (Reprinted from Institute of Southeast Asian Studies. Ed. *Southeast Asian Affairs*. [London: Heinemann Educational Books. 1979]).

Hobsbawm, Eric. 'Some Reflections on "The Break-up of Britain."' *New Left Review*, 105 (September–October 1977).

— *The Age of Revolution, 1789–1848*. New York: Mentor. 1964.

Hoffman, John. 'A Foreign Investment: Indies Malay to 1901.' *Indonesia*, 27 (April 1979). pp. 65–92.

Hughes, Christopher. *Switzerland*. New York: Praeger. 1975.

Ieu Koeus. *Pheasa Khmer. La Langue Cambodgienne (Un Essai d'etude raisonné)* Phnom Penh: n.p. 1964.

Ignotus, Paul. *Hungary.* New York and Washington, D.C.: Praeger. 1972.

Ileto, Reynaldo Clemeña. *Pasyon and Revolution: Popular Movements in the Philippines, 1840–1910.* Manila: Ateneo Press. 1979.

Jászi, Oscar. *The Dissolution of the Habsburg Monarchy.* Chicago: University of Chicago Press. 1929.

Kahin, George McTurnan. *Nationalism and Revolution in Indonesia.* Ithaca: Cornell University Press. 1952.

Katzenstein, Peter J. *Disjoined Partners. Austria and Germany since 1815.* Berkeley and Los Angeles: University of California Press. 1976.

Kedourie, Elie. Ed. and Intro. *Nationalism in Asia and Africa.* New York: Meridian. 1970.

Kelly, Gail Paradise. 'Franco-Vietnamese Schools, 1918 to 1938.' Ph.D thesis. University of Wisconsin. 1975.

Kemiläinen, Aira. *Nationalism: Problems Concerning the Word, the Concept and Classification.* Jyväskylä: Kustantajat. 1964.

Kirk-Greene, Anthony H. M. *Crisis and Conflict in Nigeria: A Documentary Source Book.* London: Oxford University Press. 1971.

Kohn, Hans. *The Age of Nationalism.* New York: Harper. 1962.

Kumar, Ann. 'Diponegoro (1778?–1855).' *Indonesia*, 13 (April 1972). pp. 69–118.

Luckham, Robin. *The Nigerian Military: A Sociological Analysis of Authority and Revolt, 1960–67.* Cambridge: Cambridge University Press. 1971.

Lumbera, Bienvenido. 'Tradition and Influences in the Development of Tagalog Poetry, 1570 to 1898.' Ph.D. thesis. University of Indiana. 1967.

Lyautey, Louis-Hubert-Gonzalve. *Lettres du Tonkin et de Madagascar (1894–1899).* Paris: Librairie Armand Colin. 1946.

Lynch, John. *The Spanish-American Revolutions, 1808–1826.* New York: Norton. 1973.

Mabry, Bevars D. *The Development of Labor Institutions in Thailand.* Ithaca: Cornell University, Southeast Asia Program, Data Paper No. 112. 1979.

MacArthur, Douglas. *A Soldier Speaks. Public Papers and Speeches of General of the Army Douglas MacArthur.* New York: Praeger. 1965.

Maki, John M. *Japanese Militarism, Its Cause and Cure.* New York: Knopf. 1945.

Marr, David G. *Vietnamese Tradition on Trial, 1920–1945.* Berkeley and Los Angeles: University of California Press. 1981.

Maruyama Masao. *Thought and Behaviour in Modern Japanese Politics.* London and Oxford: Oxford University Press. 1963.

Marx, Karl, and Friedrich Engels. *The Communist Manifesto.* In *Selected Works.* Moscow: Foreign Languages Publishing House. 1958. vol. I.

Masur, Gerhard. *Simon Bolivar.* Albuquerque: University of New Mexico Press. 1948.

McLuhan, Marshall. *The Gutenberg Galaxy: The Making of Typographic Man.* Toronto: University of Toronto Press. 1962.

Montesquieu, Henri de. *Persian Letters*. Trans. C. J. Betts. Harmondsworth: Penguin. 1973.

Moore, Jr., Barrington. *Social Origins of Dictatorship and Democracy. Lord and Peasant in the Making of the Modern World*. Boston: Beacon Press. 1966.

Morgan, Edward S. 'The Heart of Jefferson.' *New York Review of Books*. August 17, 1978.

Morgenthau, Ruth Schachter. *Political Parties in French-Speaking West Africa*. Oxford: Clarendon Press. 1964.

Moumouni, Abdou. *L'Education en Afrique*. Paris: Maspéro. 1964.

Musil, Robert. *The Man Without Qualities*. Trans. Eithne Wilkins and Ernst Kaiser. New York: Howard-McCann. 1953. vol. I.

Nairn, Tom. *The Break-up of Britain*. London: New Left Books. 1977.

— 'The Modern Janus.' *New Left Review*, 94 (November–December 1975). pp. 3–29. Reprinted as Chapter 9 in *The Break-up of Britain*.

'Nijs, E. Breton de'. *Tempo Doeloe*. Amsterdam: Querido. 1973.

Norman, E. Herbert. *Soldier and Peasant in Japan. The Origins of Conscription*. New York: Institute of Pacific Relations. 1943.

Orwell, George. *The Orwell Reader*. New York: Harcourt-Brace-Jovanovich. 1956.

Pal, Bipin Chandra. *Memories of My Life and Times*. Calcutta: Bipin Chandra Pal Institute. 1973.

'3349' [pseudonym for Phetsarath Ratanavongsa]. *Iron Man of Laos: Prince Phetsarath Ratanavongsa*. Trans. John B. Murdoch. Ed. David K. Wyatt. Ithaca: Cornell University, Southeast Asia Program Data Paper No. 110. 1978.

Polo, Marco. *The Travels of Marco Polo*. Trans. and ed. William Marsden. London and New York: Everyman's Library. 1946.

Pramoedya Ananta Toer. *Tjerita dari Blora*. Jakarta: Balai Pustaka. 1952.

Reid, Anthony J. S. *The Indonesian National Revolution, 1945–50*. Hawthorn, Victoria: Longman. 1974.

Renan, Ernest. 'Qu'est-ce qu'une nation?' In *Oeuvres Complètes*. Paris: Calmann-Lévy. 1947–61. vol. I. pp. 887–906.

Rizal, José. *The Lost Eden. Noli Me Tangere*. Trans. León Ma. Guerrero. Bloomington: Indiana University Press. 1961.

Roff, William R. *The Origins of Malay Nationalism*. New Haven and London: Yale University Press. 1967.

Said, Edward. *Orientalism*. New York: Pantheon. 1978.

Scherer, Savitri. 'Harmony and Dissonance. Early Nationalist Thought in Java.' M. A. thesis. Cornell University. 1975.

Seton-Watson, Hugh. *Nations and States. An Enquiry into the Origins of Nations and the Politics of Nationalism*. Boulder, Colo.: Westview Press. 1977.

Smith, Donald Eugene. *India as a Secular State*. Princeton: Princeton University Press. 1963.

Spear, Percival. *India, Pakistan and the West*, London, New York and Toronto: Oxford University Press. 1949.

Steinberg, S. H. *Five Hundred Years of Printing*. Rev. Ed. Harmondsworth: Penguin. 1966.

Storry, Richard. *The Double Patriots. A Study of Japanese Nationalism.* London: Chatto and Windus. 1957.

Strong, Charles Frederick. *Modern Political Constitutions.* 8th Rev. Ed. London: Sidgwick and Jackson. 1972.

Summers, Laura. 'In Matters of War and Socialism, Anthony Barnett would Shame and Honour Kampuchea Too Much.' *Bulletin of Concerned Asian Scholars,* 11:4 (October–December 1979). pp. 10–18.

Tickell, Paul. *Three Early Indonesian Short Stories by Mas Marco Kartodikromo (c. 1890–1932).* Melbourne: Monash University, Centre of Southeast Asian Studies, Working Paper No. 23. 1981.

Timpanaro, Sebastiano. *On Materialism.* London: New Left Books. 1975.

— *The Freudian Slip.* London: New Left Books. 1976.

Toye, Hugh. *Laos: Buffer State or Battleground.* London: Oxford University Press. 1968.

Turner, Victor. *Dramas, Fields and Metaphors. Symbolic Action in Human Society.* Ithaca: Cornell University Press. 1974.

— *The Forest of Symbols. Aspects of Ndembu Ritual.* Ithaca: Cornell University Press. 1967.

Vagts, Alfred. *A History of Militarism, Civilian and Military.* Rev. ed. New York: The Free Press. 1959.

Vandenbosch, Amry. *The Dutch East Indies: Its Government, Problems, and Politics.* Berkeley and Los Angeles: University of California Press. 1944.

Vella, Walter F. *Chaiyo! King Vajiravudh and the Development of Thai Nationalism.* Honolulu: University of Hawaii Press. 1978.

Veyra, Jaime de. *El 'Ultimo Adiós' de Rizal: estudio crítico-expositivo.* Manila: Bureau of Printing. 1946.

Williams, Raymond. 'Timpanaro's Materialist Challenge.' *New Left Review,* 109 (May–June 1978). pp. 3–17.

Wills, Gary, *Inventing America: Jefferson's Declaration of Independence.* New York: Doubleday. 1978.

Wolfe, Charles. *The Poems of Charles Wolfe.* London: Bullen. 1903.

Woodside, Alexander B. *Vietnam and the Chinese Model. A Comparative Study of Vietnamese and Chinese Government in the First Half of the Nineteenth Century.* Cambridge, Mass.: Harvard University Press. 1971.

Yabes, Leopoldo Y. 'The Modern Literature of the Philippines.' In Pierre-Bernard Lafont and Denys Lombard. Eds. *Littératures contemporaines de l'asie du sud-est.* Paris: L'Asiathèque. 1974. pp. 287–302.

Zasloff, Joseph J. *The Pathet Lao: Leadership and Organization.* Lexington, Mass: Lexington Books. 1973.

Index